RELIGION AND BUSINESS;

OR,

SPIRITUAL LIFE IN ONE OF ITS SECULAR DEPARTMENTS.

By A. J. MORRIS.

Wherever religion is a business, there will business be a religion.

LONDON:

WARD AND CO., 27, PATERNOSTER ROW.

1853.

THE Author would never have chosen the subject of this little Book, but from a sense of duty. It is not at all according to his taste; it is foreign to all the sympathies and habits of his mind. But he felt that the truth to be spoken on it is part of "the whole counsel of God" which he is bound to declare, and therefore sacrificed his own feelings to a task which he hopes will prove more profitable to others than it was pleasant to himself.

Having preached, he would not have published, upon this subject, but that scarcely any one else does. There are hosts of books on the evidences of Christianity, its doctrines, its institutions, its general moralities, but, though we are "a nation of shopkeepers," though commerce is enlarging its sphere and strengthening its spirit, though its evils are almost universally admitted, it is feared that little attention is given to it by the pulpit, and still less by the press.

The Author is aware of the imperfect and fragmentary character of his work. It is not what it might be; it is not, he ventures to think, what, in other circumstances, even he could make it. But he has long been learning the folly of not doing what is possible, because something else is impossible.

The Book, as printed, is for substance the same as when delivered—only some of the introductions to the Lectures, and all the concluding recapitulations and appeals, are omitted, as being less necessary to published than spoken addresses.

The Book is not controversial, nor doctrinal, but practical. It is addressed directly to the conscience and the life. There is no attempt at elaborate reasoning nor polished composition. The Author has tried to use "right words"—he is sure he has used faithful ones.

CONTENTS.

I.

The Secular Claim of Christianity.

Phil. iv. 8.

" Finally, brethren, whatsoever things are true, whatsoever
things are honest, whatsoever things are just, whatsoever
things are pure, whatsoever things are lovely, whatsoever things are of good report ; if there be any virtue,
and if there be any praise, think on these things."

I PROPOSE to begin, this evening, a short Course
of Lectures on " Religion and Business." It is
not with a view to popular acceptance that I have
selected this subject; not with a view of exciting
curiosity, and filling the sanctuary with an expect-
ant crowd, and affording them a pulpit entertainment. For that purpose a very different subject
would have been chosen; one, perhaps, having a
less immediate connexion with life and conscience ;
at any rate one whose novelty or difficulty might
present a finer opportunity for the exercise of ingenuity. Indeed, I can conceive of many, even
of practical themes possessing greater attractions
than the one now before us. But it is, in part, the
very thing which may make our topics distasteful

that has induced me to take them up. For truths
which are least liked are often most needed; and
principles most familiar to the understanding are
often the greatest strangers to the life. I have no
doubt at all, that the truth which I shall have to
bring out is emphatically "the present truth;"
and the truth which a minister can refuse to bring
out, in some way or other, only at his peril. May
that "God in whose hand our breath is and whose
are all our ways" graciously condescend to bless
this effort to honour and promote it !

The Gospel is not an abstraction. There is no
part of it which is intended to remain merely an
object of thought. It is its central principle—its
prime promise, that "the just shall live by faith."
To quicken a faith which shall secure a life is the
end of all its facts, and revelations, and institutions, and influences. Holy belief is its way to
holy being, the being of the whole man, the
healthy vitality and righteous exercise of all his
powers. But it is not enough that there be a
generally correct faith in the Gospel to secure
universal rightness of action. It will not do for
a man to say, " Oh ! if a man's heart is changed,
he will have a knowledge of all duties, and will
perform them. The Christian cannot live in sin.

Let there be but a principle of true grace, and all else will follow, morality and godliness will always go together." This is true to a certain extent, but the doctrine requires discrimination and limitation. A man may be godly in the main, and yet he may not be acquainted with all his obligations, nor, knowing them, may he discharge them. Universal observation proves the possibility of moral ignorance and moral weakness being allied to some measure of spirituality. Men have lived in all ages, and all societies, who have had the fear of God within them, and have, nevertheless, not detected their duty in all things, nor done it—yea, have lived in the constant performance of acts contradicted by the spirit and letter of Christianity. However it may be accounted for, so it is. The judgment is unenlightened or the will is feeble. Men, good men, need to have their duty pointed out, general principles they are unable to apply,—they need to have their duty enforced,—and one reason, doubtless, why so many live in systematic neglect of Christian moralities is to be found in the absence of particular instruction in them. The public ministry is often too much confined to the generalities of truth and privilege and law, leaving a large number of

minds in darkness as to the things to which
these are to be applied, and the manner of their
application. It is possible to be delighted with a
doctrine, and yet have no just conception of its
practical bearings; to revel in the thought of a
blessing, and yet not discern its exact and full
force as a moral motive; to have an intense admi-
ration of the principles of equity and love, and
yet be a stranger to both the theory and practice
of them in the varied relations of life and the
world. The illustration of the Gospel cannot be
complete unless it be specific; its enforcement must
be defective if it be not particular. This is my
reason for endeavouring to point out how the
Christian man should "walk so as to please God"
in connection with his secular pursuits.

The subject has pressing claims upon us. Business of some kind or other calls forth our powers,
and provides for our subsistence, and comforts, and
luxuries. Commerce is the condition of English
life. We cannot depend on the spontaneous pro-
ductions of nature, or the produce of the chase.
Work, hard, regular toil, is the law and necessity.
" By the sweat of our brow we must eat bread."
The exceptions to this rule are comparatively few
in this country, and still fewer in congregations

like our own. Composed scarcely at all of the leisure classes, there are but few belonging to them to whom the claim of secular Christianity is irrelevant. You are all directly or indirectly interested in what the Gospel says to the man of business.

I am sorry to have to add, that the theme is as necessary as appropriate. I am not one of those "murmurers" who are disposed to find only evil in our times, and to magnify it. I have not learned to preach the gospel of grumbling. My soul has no sympathy with those who foster the spirit of universal discontent,—who are never at peace but when they are at war,—whose only idea of activity is restlessness, and of progress change, —who believe that "whatever is, is wrong." I do not think, with some, that our social life is radically rotten, that all faith is dead, that every spark of nobleness has expired, that all our religion is ", putrescent cant," and all our morality hypocrisy and "sham." On the contrary, I cannot doubt, there is a goodly number among us who have a powerful and presiding sense of spiritual realities; who live a life of very simple and sincere godliness; who bring the spirit of moral heroism and martyrdom into the field of their daily works; who would rather suffer than sin; and who, in the factory, the shop, the counting-house, and the exchange, have the abiding, strengthening, sanctifying thought, "Thou, God, seest me!" But, at the same time, it is not to be denied, that there is a large amount of evil in our secular system; and that many of those who should resist it give to it the sanction of their example.

There must be something in what almost all admit, that the vices of trade are great, and general, and well-nigh irresistible; nor can we shut our eyes to the facts constantly occurring, to the instances of criminal conduct in the professors of religion, and the still more frequent violations of the holy spirit of the Gospel displayed by them. Most of you have met with cases of unblushing fraud associated with Christian profession—cases of persons who will salute you with some pious expressions, meet you with an open Bible, use seals with pious devices and mottoes, and yet inflict on you the most grievous injury, and commit the most wicked wrong. The professor who will take advantage of your simplicity or confidence, seduce by promises he cannot or does not mean to keep, and live upon the profits of your hard toil, may be often found. But to leave such, how often is the saying heard—"An honest man cannot live!" And how proverbial is the participation of saints in the wrong-doing of the times! Whose heart has not been pierced and humbled by the remark, "Your religious people are just as bad as the rest;" and even the remark, "I would sooner deal with a man of the world than with one of your professors"? Now, making all allowance for exaggeration, attributing as much as possible to the natural desire of the irreligious to find fault in the religious, and remembering that the profession of godliness makes more prominent and noticeable the inconsistencies of saints, this ought not to be. Cæsar's wife must not be *suspected*,—it is not enough to be able to defend Christians, there should be no room for attack. And the fact that such things are said, and believed so generally, clearly shews that there is something wrong— greatly wrong.

It is not exactly my business to point out the causes of this state of things. The general cause is men's corruption; but there must be other and secondary causes.

The *artificialness* of our secular life is one. We have got far beyond the point of simple intercourse. The rules applicable to the time of few wants and direct dealings are insufficient now. The more complicated the social system is, the more numerous its expedients, the more dove-tailed its parts, the more subdivided its labours, and the more extended its credits, the more difficult is the application to it of moral principles, the more easy and plausible their violation or evasion.

Another cause is the *competition* which obtains in our secular life. There is a race and battle for bread. There is a severe pressure upon strength and skill. Conscience is hardly bestead by the demands of life. There is an eager rivalry in most departments. Profits are run down to the lowest point. Ingenuity is strained to the last degree of endurance. To meet this exacting difficult condition, there is a powerful temptation to sacrifice at least high moral considerations. Honesty is often martyrdom. They who have not the spirit of martyrs will, therefore, often fall.

But I must avow my belief, that another cause is to be found in the too prevailing thought or feeling, *that religion and business are two distinct things*; that they belong to different departments, and have different rules and principles. It has been a mighty mischief, that religion has been so often divorced from the other modes and ways of human

life. Men have looked at it as something distinct
and peculiar, having its own sphere and its own
powers, and not as the fountain and 'father of all
goodness and truth. The man of God has been
separated from the man of science, the man of
literature, the man of politics, the man of business. The world has helped the separation, and
so has the Church. A weak and ignorant piety, a
strong and shrewd impiety, have done the same
work. The general exercises of the intellect, the
common charities of the heart, the familiar proceedings of the life, have been too frequently regarded as provinces into which religion has no
right to penetrate, or should come only when in-
vited, and be thankful to be treated as a guest, and
not expect to be honoured as a sovereign. Hence
literature, art, social life, worldly engagements,
have been treated as things apart from godliness,
and not as things which godliness is to possess,
and through which it is to act and to be seen. To
borrow an expressive illustration, the partnership
has been dissolved between religion and other
things, and thus it has come to a disastrous bankruptcy. This evil has largely prevailed in the
department of which we speak to-night. That
it has so prevailed is apparent from the fact, that

there is a general disposition to regard immoralities connected with money matters in a different
light from other immoralities. The same standard
is not applied. The same measure is not meted
out. There is a more gentle treatment of the
pecuniary sinner than of any other sinner. "It
is only in the way of business," covers a multitude
of sins. A man, in many circles, had better defraud his creditors than deny a single article of
the popular creed, or violate a single convention-
alism of respectable society.

But it is time to leave these general remarks.
So much seemed necessary in the way of introduc-
tion. What remains of our time this evening will
be devoted to a consideration of "the secular
claim of Christianity" — the manner in which
Christianity bears upon business,—to an answer
to the question, How and why should it affect and
govern our secular life? I shall, in giving this
answer, content myself with the illustration of one
thought—a thought already briefly expressed.

Religion, we have said, is *a life*. This is its
frequent and most appropriate term. It is the
highest and strongest kind of life; the noblest in
nature and mightiest in force. Every man who
is truly godly has been made to live anew—to live

toward God. He has been quickened by the Holy
Ghost. He has been born again. He has been
brought into a new connection with the Great
Spirit of all. God has become a reality to him.
God has become a reality in him. The character
of God, the will of God, the love of God, the
glory of God, have come to be potent and presiding truths in his soul. And the result of this is
a new, a better, a larger being; another kind of
existence, a holier and a fuller one. He has
received an energizing and sanctifying influence.
He is "created in Christ Jesus unto good works."
He is renewed after the image of the Holy God.
Now, in this fact of *life*, you have a clue to the
whole relations and powers of religion; and its connection with business will be sufficiently expounded
by a brief contemplation of the import of this fact.
What is life, and what does it do? This is the
question I wish you to ask. The answer to
this question will illustrate "the secular claim of
Christianity."

Life permeates.

It flows through its subject. It pervades every
part. It is not something confined and local,
whose bounds depend on your appointment or
volition. It is a spontaneous principle,—of itself,

and by means of the close communion of the parts
of organized systems, it takes possession of the whole
man, and endows him throughout with the power
of motion and sensibility. If any portion of his
frame be not so endowed there must be disease,—
if it cannot feel or act, its condition must be morbid. So it ought not to be; and, in a healthy subject, so it would not be. Now this is precisely the
case with spiritual life—this is one of the clearest
of its facts. The purest and most powerful of
vitalities, its function is to diffuse itself through the
entire being. And this it will do, if there be not
disease. If it be restricted in its flow, if it be
defective in its operations, the cause must be found
in unsoundness of the parts or a general feebleness
of the principle. And so we say, that the business
of a living spirit, a spirit living in holiness and in
God, will be naturally possessed and penetrated by
grace. There may be a defective judgment im-
peding the course of life,—the life itself may be
weak and infirm,—in such cases there will be more
or less of secular exemption from its power. But
if there be not these causes of partiality and im-
perfection, the godliness of a man will freely flow
through all his secular works and intercourses—
will do so as a life—cannot help doing so. Apart

from all settled purposes and distinct ideas, it will permeate his worldly being. His vital sympathy with truth and purity will baptize his proceedings of whatever kind; and, not only because he means it, or because he thinks about it, will he act from holy principles and according to holy rules, but because he lives, lives by a faith which has formed him according to those rules, and filled him with those principles. I repeat, if his religion be healthy and strong, it will not be a question whether he shall bring it into business, it will not depend on his formal intention to do so, but he will do it naturally and unconsciously, because his business is part of a system possessing life. If he do it not, it must be from the want of vital energy, or from the presence of some unnatural obstruction. The secular demand of Christianity is, therefore, in the first place, the demand that Christianity shall, as a living power, appear and operate in worldly things, giving rule, motion, and aim to common daily works, breathing a spirit of sanctity into the forms of the most mechanical and familiar pursuits of life. If Christianity be enlightened and vigorous, it must thus prevail. Only on the supposition of ignorance or feebleness can its failure be accounted for.

Life resists.

While it is diffusive, it is repellent. Physical life has a great force in overcoming injurious agencies. Living things can, to a great extent, withstand the action of destructive elements, or can repair its effects. The living plant, the living animal, the living man, can bear what would have a sudden and surprising operation on the dead, or can recover from that operation. And spiritual life reveals its power in bidding defiance to influences that overcome the irreligious soul. Its office is seen in withstanding the attacks of evil, and in recovering from their temporary impressions. It is essentially defensive and conservative. It is not meant to yield to the sinful powers that are in the world, but to vanquish them.

Thus, if it be alleged, that secular life is unfriendly to the soul's welfare, that the pursuits of business have a bad tendency,—we answer, the principle of religion is designed to counteract it. We grant, that there is much in worldly things, in incessant toil, and in the present condition of commerce, to corrupt and deaden the heart. But here is the sphere and function of godliness. They will harden the carnal,—they are to be resisted by the spiritual. There is no need for

one who has the higher life to fall before them.
It is part of his vocation and a mode of his
vitality to oppose the besetting sinfulness.

It would be impossible to illustrate all the ways
in which religion should operate to the conser-
vation of the spirit. But call to mind the chief
methods of its general influence, and apply them
to the subject in hand.

We cannot read the Bible without seeing that
the spirit of martyrdom is the spirit of the Gospel.
Now this spirit may be displayed in commerce
just as truly as at the stake, or in the prison.
To suffer for the name of Jesus is not the portion
only of those that are persecuted, it is also of
those that are tempted. We may be called to
endure just as much to preserve our purity as our
faith; just as much in doing as in professing the
Gospel. It is nothing to say, that " If we retain
our integrity, we shall lose our trade,"—there have
been thousands who could say, " If we retain our
faith, we shall lose our lives." The same principle that makes it right and noble for a man to
testify for Christ at the expense of liberty and
existence makes it right and noble for a man to
obey Christ at the expense of pecuniary profit and
even the means of subsistence.

C

The preserving power of religion appears *in keeping us out of temptation* as well as in resisting it when it comes. We have no right to subject ourselves to the powerful solicitations of sin. If, therefore, business be of such a kind that it necessitates our wrong-doing, our religion should prompt us to abstain from it. If it be sure to bring us into perils that it is scarce possible for us to withstand, the voice of principle commands us away. Or, if a certain amount of business engagements— a certain intensity of secular pursuits—be incompatible with spirituality, we must withhold ourselves. Here, perhaps, is the most frequent failure of men. They do not ruin themselves so often by their evil practices in the way of business, as by an excessive devotion to it. They give to it an amount of time, and thought, and feeling, totally inconsistent with the due cultivation of the heart,— they surround themselves with a worldly atmosphere in which it is impossible for the spirit to breathe well and healthily,—they burden themselves with work and care and responsibility that prevent all free and noble action of the higher powers. Some do it complainingly, bewailing all the time the difficulty of due attention to the things of God. And many do it from no call of necessity—though that would be no justification—but simply from a desire and determination to be rich, for the sake of large possessions, of rivalling their neighbours, or of leaving a pernicious legacy to their children. To all this religion administers a severe rebuke. It says, Keep out of temptation,—expose not thy soul to ruin,—go not in the evil way,—deny thyself,—guard against the excessive pursuit of the lawful,—beware how the innocent degenerates into the sinful,—and expect not the preserving power of God while thou art wilfully or heedlessly rushing into danger. And, so far as it is a living force within us, its power will appear in our obedience to its counsels.

Life subordinates.

It has a great strength in making things minister to its nourishment. That which is injurious it resists, that which is not so it appropriates, extracting virtue from it, assimilating it to its own nature. Now spiritual life does this also. We are not to look on business as itself sinful. It may become so. There are sinful businesses, and sinful degrees of lawful businesses, and sinful ways of doing lawful businesses; but business is not sinful in its own nature. It is a natural vocation, a divine appointment, a duty, a privilege. And religious life is intended to use it for religious purposes. The least thing in it is its exercise of our powers. An idle soul is in imminent peril of becoming a sinful soul. Multitudes have been ruined by having nothing to do—no regular and wholesome employment for their faculties. But business may *directly* minister to a man's spirituality, if that spirituality be vigorous and wise. It is more than something to be resisted—it is something to be employed. The active play of holy dispositions is strengthening, and business is the chief sphere in most men's lives for their exercise. To bring principle into plan and purpose,—to bring Gospel estimates to bear on worldly gains, and Gospel comforts to bear on worldly losses,—to infuse its spirit into intercourse with men,—to sanctify the suggestive power of things and persons by the laws of spiritual association,—all these and many other things help to make business a nourisher and strengthener of the holy life. We must not content ourselves with a victory over business, with a successful opposition to its temptations and insensible influences, with getting no harm from it. A higher triumph awaits us as the spiritual children of the Most High. After vanquishing it as a foe, we must. use it as a servant. It may be a discipline, a lesson, a means of grace. It was to the

shepherds watching their flocks by night that the
angel of the Lord announced the birth of the Mes-
siah. It was by a star that the wise men of the
East, who studied astronomy, were led to the babe
in Bethlehem. In these cases, God consecrated
the ordinary pursuits of inquirers after truth to
bring them to the knowledge of incarnate good, and
even so now the spiritual man may prove that it is
not in the neglect of his daily work, but in it, and
by it, the soul can be nourished by the grace of
Christ. It is no common attainment—but it is a
possible one. There is nothing in it foreign to life.
It is a natural mode of its exercise. If life in us
be enlightened and energetic, we shall rejoice in this
subordination of the secular to the spiritual.

Life propagates.

It can and does reproduce itself, perpetuates and
multiplies itself; and, even much more than physical life, has spiritual life this power. Now, this
is the last way in which business is connected with
religion—in which religion has a claim upon business. Even spiritual good is not enough if it be
our own exclusively. The work and intercourse
of the world should be used as a form and instrument of spiritual life to others. It is one of the
things—and often the only thing—in which our

godliness can come before men—the only thing in which they have an opportunity of seeing what we are as the people of the Lord. They cannot see us in the closet; they cannot see us in the family; they cannot see us in the church; but they do see us in our secular affairs. They have the means of judging of us in them. And what a means! How important this test! It comes close to them. It touches them in the most sensitive part. They can appreciate commercial morality. However unable to understand the articles of our faith, or to feel the force of high spiritual appeals, they can instantly detect the practical worth of a godliness revealed in the things of this world—the virtues and graces that make the honest, truthful, trustworthy man of business. Paul told servants to "adorn the doctrine of God their Saviour" in their conduct to their masters; and if it was possible, in their humble life, to exhibit and commend the word of Christ, how earnestly may you be exhorted to do so in the engagements and intercourses of secular life? How many have been permanently prejudiced against religion by seeing and suffering from the unrighteous conduct of those who have named the name of Christ? And how many have been first led to value and inquire after

Gospel truth from beholding its silent influence chastening and governing its disciples in the daily doings of the world? If unbelieving husbands may, "without the word," as Peter speaks, "be won by the conduct of the wives," irreligious men of business may be won, without the word, by the conduct of their brethren having the faith of Jesus. And it is written, "Let your light so shine before men, that they may see your good works, and glorify your Father who is in heaven."

II.

The Christian at his Work.

ROM. XII. 11.

" Not slothful in business."

OUR subject to-night is, "The Christian at his
work." It takes in every kind of work—from the
lowest and most mechanical labour up to the
most strenuous employment of the intellect, and
the most self-denying exercises of disinterested
charity. Every Christian ought to be a worker.
If he were not one before he became a Christian,
Christianity should have made him one. There
are none present, then, to-night, to whom our
subject should be inapplicable. There is something wrong, if you be mere listeners to what is
said to others. If you be, I pray God that what
is spoken may be blessed not only to their guidance and sanctification, but to the quickening,
and shaming, and stimulating of yourselves!

As to workers, there is a grievous heresy about.
That heresy is involved in the common mode of
employing the phrase, "the working classes." It

is false and fulsome; for it is just as possible to be sycophantic to the poor as to the rich—to be adulators of the low as of the high. Who are meant by "the working classes?" One class—the class of manual workers, the labourers, and mechanics, the men of skilled and unskilled physical toil. And by the application of the term to them, as a distinctive and exclusive appellation, it is quietly assumed that all other classes are idlers, that they do nothing, that they are cumberers of the ground, consumers of the unearned produce of other men's toil. Nothing can be more erroneous and injurious than this assumption. It may be very flattering to the class so described, and may serve the purpose of those who would use that class for their own ends, but it is either a mistake or a trick. "The working classes" include very many besides those destined to the drudgery of material labour. Most of the middle class and many of the upper are workers also. The tradesman, the merchant, the professional man, the artist, the author, the magistrate, the statesman, are all workers.

The vice of this favourite phrase, as generally used, appears also in the fact, that while a portion only of the community are described as if they worked, the work done by that portion is, however necessary, not the highest kind of work. We cannot, of course, do without food, and raiment, and shelter; the industry which makes available for use the fruits of the earth, and the treasures hid beneath it, lies at the base of material life, but there are many things greater and better nevertheless. No one disesteems life—physical life,— "all that a man hath will he give for his life,"— but there are yet many nobler endowments than life. What life is to the graces of life and the powers of life and the sanctities of life, that is the industry which sustains life to the other and higher industries of man. Because the foundation is indispensable to the building, we must not think more of him that lays it than of those whose scientific skill and artistic taste conceive and fashion the majestic superstructure. Surely there is some greatness and worthiness in the labour by which facts are formed into theories, and mighty thoughts are worked out, and things of beauty are breathed forth, and laws are enacted and executed, and the complete system of social life is preserved and sustained, and the manifold influences of Christian truth and human charity are brought to bear on the ignorant, the wretched, and the depraved. It is a low materialism that is couched in the expression, as it is commonly employed, of "the working classes." It puts a part for the whole, and it ignores the noblest spheres and orders of human labour.

Be it understood, then, that to-night I do not address some workers only, but all. Whatever the scene, the nature, the instruments of your service, my word is to you. And may God give you all grace to receive and obey the truth!

I. *"The Christian at his work" may feel that work is a good and noble thing.*

Christianity does greatly honour honest industry. There may be those who feel ashamed of any contact with it, who would rather be suspected of crime than of labour, especially the labour of the hands. There are such, if report be true. But *from the Bible they get no sanction.* God does not approve their thought. There are two Testaments, and both shed a glory on faithful and laborious toil. Of our race there have been two heads—the natural and the spiritual, the first man and the second, Adam and the Lord from heaven. The one was a gardener in Paradise, the other a carpenter in Nazareth. The two sinless, the two freshest from the hands of God, the two springs

of human being, have taught us, thus, that whatever our descent, whatever our character, whatever
our relations, Christians may feel it no dishonour
to be at work.

*There is a natural voice of self-respect whose
tones Christianity deepens and empowers.*

It is honourable *to be independent.* The more
there is of self in our portion the more blessed
and glorious it is. The more of our own energy
and life it contains the more precious ; in a word,
the more our own it is. For things are made ours
not so much by communication to us as communication from us. In the highest sense, and
for the highest uses, that is most mine, not which
is most given to me, but which has received most
from me. The deepest kind of possession belongs
to objects not bestowed by others, but wrought out
by a man's own activity. And, therefore, it is a
glorious feeling which a man has when, by his own
assiduity and toil, he provides from himself for
himself. He may fall short of the property of
others who have not laboured for it—he may be
without their broad acres, and ample incomes, and
civil honours, but if there be less for him to
possess, he possesses it more. He has feelings
which a " stranger " to his labours cannot " inter-

meddle with," a boasting which no man can stop, that he is more to himself than any other is, that what he has he has made, that he receives what he has given, reaps what he has sown. And, thus, all the enjoyments and powers of life, beyond their intrinsic value, have the sweet and noble quality of rewards. There is no disgrace in deriving riches and renown from ancestors, but there is virtue and glory in obtaining them from ourselves, and that religion which makes everything of the will and nothing of accidents, which aims ever at deepening personal interest and impressing personal responsibility, smiles ineffably at "the Christian at his work."

Most important is the exercise of the faculties.

The value of daily toil of some kind is in this, that it prevents the evils of stagnation, the wretched results of indolence. Activity is the law of nature ; everything that has life and health is meant to be active. Everything can preserve these blessings in their fulness only by being active. And here comes in the blessedness of the ordinance of labour—the benevolence of the law that to eat men must work. True, somewhat of its value is destroyed by the very perfection to which we have attained. The extreme division of

labour which obtains among us, with all its great
and many advantages, has this sore disadvantage,
that it tends to a partial development of faculty—
an undue growth of particular powers; but this
cannot be helped; it is inseparable from an ad-
vanced condition of society, and, after all, one
faculty cannot be used alone. The necessity
of work is generally a blessing. It quickens,
strengthens, refreshes, occupies, and cleanses the
mind and body. It is even needful to those who
might, without it, not be quiescent. The merely
meditative often go wrong. Speculative thought,
alone, is apt to be partial or unsound. Many have
fallen into wretched theories and more wretched
moods, because the thinking powers have not been
yoked to their active energies. If the "vision" of
life is made plain, that "he may run that readeth
it," it is also true, in a sense, that he only can
read it who runs. The most healthy and the
safest condition is that in which a regular and
moderate demand is made for toil. It exerts a
sanitary and stimulating influence upon the general
disposition and power to work. It is a remarkable
fact, and yet not remarkable, that many of those
who have done most in departments of strictly
voluntary service have been those who had most

to do in others. The best doers of extra work are
often those whose share in necessary labour is the
largest. And therefore we say, that Christianity
which seeks the maturity and wholesome state of
our nature looks benignly on "the Christian at his
work."

*Christianity, in elevating man, elevates his en-
gagements.*

It cares comparatively little for the sphere and
form of our outward life, but attaches every importance to its spirit and its power. It is a false
judgment which estimates human worth and dignity according to the rank and style of the physical
lot. The great canon is, "as a man is, so is his
strength." And so is everything else, his peace,
his honour, and his power. It is the "good man"
that makes the good deed, the great man that
makes the great deed. You do little, in the Christian sense, to magnify or purify a man by changing
the mode of his service; you do everything by
changing its spirit. The daily business may be a
poor and paltry thing in itself; the labour of the
hands may seem, to the worldly eye, degrading;
but it is so only when we look at the worker
through the work, and not at the work through
the worker. The worker is more than the work;

and it is as he is. The question, in so far as secular deeds are concerned, is not, what I do, but what I am who do it. Life is as letters—the same letters may convey profoundest wisdom and absurdest folly. A slave, according to Paul, may do his work "unto the Lord," and make a divine service of his hard drudgery. It is as a mode of expressing the active principles of spiritual godliness, as a glass and weapon of the soul, that I must regard my secular occupation; and, therefore the Gospel, which makes everything of what a man is, and raises and refines him, constituting him a servant and a child of God, changing the character though it may not alter the form of his worldly lot and business, has only words of impressive approbation for " the Christian at his work."

II. *The Christian at his work may feel that he is filling the sphere intended for him.*

He is not only doing what, in general, is worth doing, but he is, or he may be, able to realize the design and appointment of God in his own department of service. God has made work a noble thing; and he has ordained the manner and mode of his work. He is in his right place. That is, the Bible teaches a present providence as well as an original ordinance in reference to work. It teaches, that a man may be quite sure of the intention of God, that he should be where he is, and do what he does. God appoints our lot, and chooses our inheritance for us; and his voice in the Gospel is, "Let every man wherein he is called therein abide with God."

Of course, this doctrine of providence is not the doctrine of fatalism. We are not so to think of God's appointment as if it interfered with our free agency, or released us from responsibility. "Whatever is, is right," so far as it is done by God; but it may be wrong, so far as it is done by us. A man must not say, "Here I am, in a certain state, and surrounded by certain circumstances; God has placed me here; and here I must remain. It is true that I am following an unlawful calling; but, as all things are of God, that must be of God. If I endeavoured to get out of it, I should be going against his will." A Christian man will not, cannot so speak. It is true that, in a sense, we cannot frustrate God's purpose; we cannot resist his power. It is true that all things are foreseen and permitted by God, when not appointed. It is true that God will bring his purposes to pass, even by means of man's wickedness.

But there is a limit, not to providence, but to our right of inferring our duty from its ordinations and permissions. Our worldly lot may be a matter of volition. We need not stay in a state which necessitates transgression. If we cannot live without sinning, it is a sin to live.

It is, then, our business to ascertain the will of God in reference to our worldly pursuits. It may be done. That which is presented to us,—that which we are fitted for,—that to which we are directed by circumstances,—these are the evidences, interpreted by a just and godly spirit. If a man really bring a good conscience to the task, and earnestly seek God's direction; if he do his best to obtain divine counsel, and then do his best to detect it; if he "direct his prayer unto God, and look up"; if he unite the dependent heart with the clear eye; there need be no great mistake as to the scene and sphere in which God means him to live and labour.

Of course, the calling must be *a lawful one*. This is an essential condition. A man must be satisfied of this before he can take comfort from the thought, that he is "in his place." It would be impossible for me to point out which are, and which are not, lawful callings. As a general rule,

it is not difficult for any Christian to distinguish
them. He who wishes to be right may be so.
Most difficulties here, as elsewhere, arise not from
the dimness of the duty but the perverseness of
the will. The difficulty is often, not in finding
out the right, but in making the wrong right. It
is easy enough to discover the proper course but not
so easy to prove that the improper course is the
proper one. There are, doubtless, cases of moral
perplexity. We have met with such; but they
are cases of perplexity, not so much because of
what a man is himself required to do, as because
of the connection of what he does with others. If
a man cannot pursue his calling without violating
the law of God, his course is plain. But the
question occurs, How far is he responsible for what
others may do? Should he furnish them with the
means and opportunities of sinning? That is a
more difficult question. It seems clear that in
no instance can a man be justified by the fact,
that if he do not a wrong thing, others will. For
others he is not responsible, but for himself. This
argument would justify almost anything. If all
men do wrong, that is no excuse for us. Nor is it
any excuse for us if quite as much wrong will be
done, whether we do it or not. Duty is irre-

spective of the question, whether its performance
will diminish the amount of disobedience in others.
We are accountable for our actions in themselves,
and for our moral example. Nor may we ask
Cain's question, "Am I my brother's keeper?"
The Gospel teaches us that we are. If, therefore,
a trade consist in furnishing what is known or
believed to be only evil, and to be capable only of
an evil use, a Christian man may not pursue it.
For instance:—I do not believe in the essential
sinfulness of war, but if I did, I could not with a
good conscience make guns and cannon-balls; I
cannot see the essential sinfulness of all artificial
stimuli, but if I did, I could not be a brewer or
a publican. But when it comes to be a question,
whether men may or may not make a good use of
the products of a business, then the case is different. For instance:—A Christian bookseller will
not sell a bad book, a book sure to do harm, and
only harm, but there are many books, not bad in
themselves, which may fall into the hands of those
who will make a bad use of them. Is he to refuse
to sell? I think not. He cannot be answerable
for the consequences of folly and sin. There is
nothing which may not be perverted. It would
put an end to all business if no man did what

could not be abused. For there is nothing incapable of abuse. The Gospel itself is "a savour of death unto death."

But supposing a man to have exercised a prayerful spirit and a good conscience on the point before us, supposing him to be engaged in a lawful calling, and one pointed out by circumstances for him, then we say he may feel that he is filling a divine sphere. He may feel at his work that he is where God intends him to be. In other words, it is a "calling"—a divine vocation—as much so as if he had heard the voice of God summoning him to his place of labour, or had seen the finger of God pointing him to it. He may feel not only that he should be doing something, but that he should be doing what he is about, not only that he should be somewhere in God's field or factory, but that he should be where he is. And he ought to feel this. And he will never rise to the true elevation of his work, he will never realize its proper dignity, he will never bring to it the right spirit, he will never experience all the encouraging and ennobling considerations with which it is connected, till he does feel it.

Is it not a soul-inspiring thought, for any toiler in this hard world, "I am doing the work of my

Heavenly Father "? It is not the nature of the service, but the being that is served, that gives importance to it. Men have rejoiced in spreading their richest garments beneath the feet of royalty, not degraded by the deed, but honoured by its object. And if I can connect my worldly occupation with a divine will, and engage in it as one " serving the Lord; " if I can look on it as a mode of accomplishing the pleasure of Him who is the Sovereign of the universe and of my soul; if I can feel that, however humble the scene and the instruments of my secular vocation, I am as truly discharging a trust and filling an office assigned to me by God as a king upon a throne, or even as his angel messengers; shall I not give myself to labour in the spirit of a holy ambition, and hear the command to be " not slothful in business," as a summons to glory as well as an obligation to toil?

III. *Christianity will exert a direct and powerful influence on the Christian at his work.*

It will regulate it.

I mean especially that he will make his work subservient to his godliness. He will not permit himself to be so engrossed with it as to hinder the higher work of eternal redemption. That is, so far as he is a Christian, he will not. Work is a bless-ing; but it may become a curse. Excess spoils all things. "Much honey," says Solomon, "is not good."

It is quite necessary that even lawful business should have its limits and intermissions. Speaking spiritually, it is good only with something else. It has to the direct means of spiritual growth the re-lations of exercise to food. Exercise is healthy; but it is no substitute for nourishment. Work is spiritually healthy; but it is no substitute for immediate fellowship with truth and God. The world will never be sanctified by him who neglects the church. The strength for the life is obtained in the closet.

In this light, what a blessing is the Sabbath! It is, to take the lowest view, the drag-chain on the wheels of the soul on its secular incline. It is, to take the highest view, the replenishing it with power from on high. As connected with rest and with religion, it is one of the most precious boons of heaven. And I confess that, taking this view of the Sabbath, I look with great dismay at the tendency of our times, and with surprise and sorrow at the course taken by many professed patriots and Christians. The opening, on that day,

of places of public recreation and amusement, and
that by express legislative sanction and approval,
cannot but be a matter of deep regret to those who
have no faith in their sanctifying and but little in
their moralizing influence; who think that the
substitution of sculptures for sermons, and paint-
ings for preachings, which substitution is sure to
result in innumerable instances, can do no good
but only harm to souls; and who expect and fear
that the inroads thus made on the British Sunday,
professedly for the sake of the poor, will lead
ultimately to the loss of the day to them altogether. I am not an advocate for the Jewish
Sabbath, and I by no means agree with all that is
said against the movement in favour of the opening
on Sunday, of the Crystal Palace, but I see, or
think I see, that things are tending to the intro-
duction among us of the continental Sunday,
which none would have so much reason to lament
as the poor, in whose name it is sought to be done.
The thin edge of the wedge is being inserted, the
thick one may follow. What is begun in pleasure
may end in work. Merriment often terminates
in tears.

I must also say, that Christianity should make
us endeavour to abridge the labouring hours, when

excessive, of our brethren as well as our own.   It
is beyond all dispute that the excessive toil of multitudes is, if not fatal to religion, a terrific obstacle
to it.   Surely the time will come, if the Gospel is
to maintain its character and be "glad tidings" to
the people, when man will not always be doomed
to work for life and never live; to fill up his whole
time with the painful and monotonous slavery of
his lower powers, leaving his higher in sleep or
paralysis; to devote his morning, noon, and night
to a struggle for mere existence, using, if he use
them at all, his noblest faculties only as means of
maintaining it.   What can be done is not now
before us,—but the Gospel will, some day, have
something to say about that, if it have not now.
One thing at least can be done.   There is no
earthly need why the thousands who serve in our
shops should not be earlier released from their
daily service.   It is proved that their long hours
injure body, soul, and spirit; and without the shadow of a reason are those long hours maintained.
A great part of the remedy for this state of things
is with the public, and especially the female public.
If they would discountenance the system by their
example, if they would conscientiously make their
purchases before a certain hour, when they can

see better and suffer less, they would do much for the redemption, every way, of multitudes whose plaintive cry is, "Care ye not that we perish?"

The Christian at his work may be with God.

"Let every man wherein he is called *therein abide with God.*" There is no necessity for the exclusion of religious things from the mind during secular engagements. Some afford more and better opportunities for their entertainment than others, but all afford some. It is a strange occupation which has no intervals, no hours, or minutes, or moments of intermission; and to fill these with Christian meditations and prayers is the great privilege of the saint. Before king Artaxerxes, Nehemiah "prayed unto the God of heaven." And who of us may not interweave holy thoughts and ejaculatory supplications with manual or mental work? I fear that many fail here, and suffer for it. Vastly important is it thus to keep up the sense and savour of the spiritual; to maintain the unity of our religious life; and to put a frequent check upon the inroads of worldly love and care. It is more important to be often dealing thus with God and his Gospel than to observe distant seasons of prolonged spiritual exercises; but, when both are done, the strength and delicacy of divine principle are best preserved and increased.

A mind thus kept spiritual will be able to make some use of work for the purposes of the soul. How much of the carnality of worldly things, which we lament, is owing to our own want of a fresh and lively grace? How much more would they be to us if we were more to them? How many water-pots are there in our earthly life, which, if filled by us with water, would be filled by Christ with wine? We have to do with *men*. What a field of profitable thought is human nature —at work, toiling, joying, sorrowing, gaining, losing, scheming, struggling? To a spiritual mind, what a text for comment! What lessons of humility, gratitude, sympathy, compassion, come from the labouring world to a soul possessing the truth of the Gospel! What illustrations and confirmations of the sayings and sentiments of this universal book! But we have to do with *things*. And these are *suggestive*. Objects, places, times, all may be yoked to the soul's chariot. They cannot be meaningless to human souls. And if we associated them with spiritual things, if we dealt with them with hearts filled with the Spirit, what hints and remembrances would they furnish! Nor

is this all. Things are *symbolic* as well as suggestive. Such is the harmony of worlds, such the
unity that obtains in the earthly and heavenly
spheres, that we may always find figures in the
lowest callings of objects and laws belonging to
the kingdom of God. He who has put his lessons
of divinest wisdom into parables taken from agri-
culture and commerce has taught us how we may
make the scenes and instruments and processes of
our secular labour the mirrors and voices of most
spiritual truth.

Not only may the Christian at his work be with
God, *but God may be with him.*

It is written, " Acknowledge the Lord in all thy
ways, and he shall direct thy steps." What right
have we to limit this promise? I believe that it
covers our theme, and that the Christian may seek
and obtain the guidance of divine counsel in the
prosecution of his humblest service. And there
are many who can testify that God has not left
them without the help of his suggestions when engaged in their daily toil.

And if the guidance of God may be had, his
prospering blessing may be had also. " The blessing of the Lord, it maketh rich, and He addeth no
sorrow with it." God has not promised to succeed

all our plans. He may be pleased to disappoint them, but the Christian may rejoice that God will do what is best to be done. And how often does He manifestly interpose for the relief and the advancement of His people!

And may there not be the presiding sense of the divine love, "the love of God shed abroad in the heart," whatever the course of providential events, giving strength in adversity, and infusing a nobler joy in prosperity? This is the blessed portion of the highly spiritual, to hear the still small voice saying, "I am with thee!" What a quickener of faculty, what an energizer of will, is this? Well may that man go singing to his work, whose heart is "kept by the peace which passeth all under-standing."

III.

The Christian in Commerce.

NEH. v. 15.

"But so did not I, because of the fear of God."

NEHEMIAH did not what "the former governors" did. They had been "chargeable unto the people." This was not necessarily wrong; but as he was rich, out of compassion to the condition of the people, he did it not from a principle of divine reverence. If "the fear of God" should sometimes keep from the doing of what is lawful—from the exaction of legal claims, much more should it keep from the doing of what is unlawful—from the exaction of illegal claims. It is a noble sight to see a man, moved simply from religious considerations, departing from customs sanctioned by society, going against the tide of opinion and practice, foregoing worldly profits, deaf to the pleas that satisfy the multitude, insensible to the influences that mould and rule them, meekly asserting a spiritual independence, silently rebuking the sinfulness and servility of the times, only careful of acquitting himself to God, and realizing his ideal of moral integrity. He is like a spring of water in an arid desert. He is like a star shining brightly amidst dark clouds.

I have chosen the words as my motto to-night, because of the form which the religion of commerce must necessarily take among us. Our subject is, "The Christian in Commerce," and one of the aspects and operations of godliness most required by the state of commerce is resistance. If the Christian man would describe his business dealings with others, he must often, in reference to prevailing habit, say, "So did not I because of the fear of God." The greatest difficulties in the way of a thoroughly Christian commercial life arise out of the practices which largely obtain. The enforcement of right conduct is met by an appeal to general sanction, and a reference to the consequences which would follow from its adoption, in ridicule and condemnation, in loss and suffering. "It can't be wrong for it is always done," "If I did not so, I should be laughed at for over-scrupularity," "It would be impossible to carry on business, or, at least with a profit, in any other way." And thus, the Christian tradesman must assume the attitude of Nehemiah. His principles must take the shape of reform and opposition. He must be prepared to be singular, to act out the dictates of conscience without reference to the maxims and matters of men, to say, "So do not I because of the fear of God."

Our last lecture, "The Christian at his Work," properly includes our present one, as commerce is the work of multitudes, their daily task. But if it is work, it is work of such a kind as to deserve separate consideration. For it has this property, that it brings men into contact with each other,— its very essence is intercourse and interchange; and, therefore, it is worthy of distinct contemplation, not only on account of its importance, but on account of the peculiar duties and temptations arising from its nature. It is obvious that work, which consists in the carrying on of dealings with our fellow-men, must be very different in its responsibilities and perils from work pursued in private, or merely in the presence of others. At the same time, I do not confine myself, to-night, to those whose whole business is barter. Commerce is the necessity of all. We live by exchange. And my remarks will therefore have reference to every individual before me.

Very great is the change which has passed upon society since the only commerce consisted in the

exchange by one man of what he had made or
caught for something which another had made or
caught; when the produce of the chase, or the
rude manufactures of untrained skill were its
only materials, and direct barter its only mode.
Perhaps, it could not well be removed from this
state further than it is at present, when trade has
attained to the perfection of a system, and credit
is an essential element of it.   It is no longer the
simple exchange, on a rough calculation, of the
merest necessaries of life by those who have made
or those who have taken them, but maker, merchant,
broker, and retail dealer, are all concerned in trans-
mitting to the consumer, in a form fit for use,
materials brought by the ingenuity of a score of
minds, and the industry of a hundred hands, into
their last and perfect state, for which payment is
made through the media of conventional representatives of value, which are not always immediately
paid, but secured by notes, promises, or the good
credit of estate and character.   The consequence
of this is, as I observed in my first lecture, that
the application of high moral principles to commerce is rendered more difficult.   Greater facilities
are afforded for wrong-doing; and more powerful
temptations to wrong-doing.   This is one of the

respects in which a high civilization is attended
with disadvantage, and men have to pay for privilege in an increase of moral difficulty and moral
risk.

I. *I shall, in the first place, endeavour to point
out what Christianity requires of a man in his
dealings in business with his fellow-men.*

*Christianity requires the most rigid adherence to
the principles of moral integrity.*

Truth is one of these. This is the basis of all
intercourse. Society would be impossible without
truth. It is one of the most obvious dictates of
conscience. It is the most natural thing. Truth
comes first and most easily before the mind,—we
have to go in quest of falsehood. It is the per-
emptory and unmistakeable claim of men. No
man thinks lying right; men may seek to excuse
it, but they cannot attempt to justify it. The
Gospel gives its solemn sanction to truth—enforces
it by its most awful authority. It is an indispensable quality of every Christian,—its absence
infallibly marks the sinner. Without it, no one
can enter heaven,—to be destitute of it is to have a
sure title to perdition.

And the truth required is a most comprehensive

virtue. It takes in far more than the literal state-
ment of the fact. There may be falsehood without its form. As it is said that the highest right
is the greatest injury, so the strictest truth may be
the greatest lie. For there are two parties concerned—the speaker and hearer—and truth consists
in a conveyance of the true impression from one to
the other. It is clear that a false impression may
be made, and may be intended to be made, while
no erroneous words pass from the lips. When
Abraham said, " She is my sister," he said what
was the fact, but it had all the effect, and was
intended to have all the effect, of a direct untruth.
For there may be concealment of part of the truth,
and a part necessary to a correct representation.
Or words may be employed which the hearer is
sure to understand in a different sense from that
of the speaker. Or the look and manner and
action may suggest another meaning than that
which the words would themselves convey. In
such cases, it is a wretched delusion to suppose
that the truth is uttered.

The application of this to the subject before us
is easy. All positive misrepresentations are condemned ; all averments that things are what they
are not, that they came from whence they came

not, that they were made by those that made them
not, that they are worth what they are not. All
the arts by which one thing is palmed off for
another, one thing exhibited in the window and
another sold in the shop, and a false appearance
given to things, now by darkness and now by
light, are condemned. All deficient scales and
measures are condemned. All pretences, when un-
founded, of " special bargains," " bankrupt stocks,"
" amazing sacrifices," " cheapest houses," " royal
patronage," are condemned. All promises which
cannot be or are not meant to be kept, and the
breaking of promises once made, are condemned.
And if the false arts of the dealer are condemned,
let not the purchaser imagine that he escapes.
The pretences that what is wanted is not wanted,
that it has been purchased more cheaply elsewhere
when it has not been, that it is very inferior to
what it really is, belong to falsehood. " It is
naught, it is naught, saith the buyer, but when
he is gone his way, then he boasteth." It is as
old as Solomon—as modern as ourselves—to de-
preciate in buying, and then boast of the cheapness
of the purchase. Is it not the every-day practice
of multitudes of professing saints?

Honesty is another Christian virtue in com-

merce. Honesty is justice—the giving of every
one his due. It involves the meeting of all equitable
claims, the fulfilment of all engagements voluntarily undertaken or assumed, the most rigid respect for the rights of property. He is a dishonest man who incurs responsibilities he cannot
meet, or declines discharging those he has incurred.

For a man to refuse to pay his debts is dishonest. He ought to pay them—ought to "owe
no man anything." He is not released from
this obligation by inability. He had no right,
knowingly, to incur debt without the ability to
pay it, and, having incurred it, he is bound to
make every effort for its discharge. What he has
is not properly his own till this be done. I know
that a hundred delicate and perplexing questions
might easily be put, in reference to actual or con-
ceivable cases, questions which perhaps I could not
answer. But I am clear and certain as to the
general principle. What a man owes is not his,
and he is bound to treat it as not his. The application of this doctrine must be left to individual
conscience and judgment. If a debtor maintain
unnecessary rank and style, and indulge in luxuries, he does so at the expense of his creditors ;
and if he gratify his benevolence by liberal gifts,

he sacrifices justice to charity. Nor is he excused by the fact, that he can do it with impunity, that his creditors are afraid, or have not the power, to compel payment. He may keep himself out of the sphere of the law; but moral equity is independent of human law, and if he have done so in order to be safe in his dishonesty, it is only an aggravation of his crime, and not a proof of his innocence. I will go further. The most solemn protection of law cannot release him. A debt is a debt until it be paid or forgiven. Bankruptcy is not a payment. It may shield from the civil consequences of debt, but it leaves its moral obligation. A man, through it, may be safe from his fellow-man, but he is accountable to God. No earthly tribunal can exempt from the claims of eternal justice; and an honest debtor will deem nothing his while his creditors are unsatisfied in fact or in feeling. It is a grand saying of De Foe, " The obligation of an honest man can never die."

But, I have said, that a man has no right to incur pecuniary liabilities he cannot meet. And an honest man will not. Our foregoing remarks apply to those who have incurred them, but justice requires that they should be avoided at any cost.

The simple rule of equity is that we may not even hazard another's property. The hope that it will not suffer is not sufficient for justification. I am bound to take as much care of what is my neighbour's as of what is my own. Yea, I am bound to take more care of it. If I choose to risk my own, I have no right to risk his. If, therefore, I incur expenses without the certainty—so far as certainty in human things is attainable—of meeting them,— if I become indebted to others, on the strength of my position and character, beyond my means, with the chance of being in a condition to satisfy their claims,—if I speculate or rather gamble with a view to great bargains, when I cannot, if those bargains be not realized, fulfil my engagements,—if I buy, in the hope of selling at a large profit, that which I cannot pay for, if the profit be not obtained,—I am guilty of dishonesty. It is nothing to say, that the men with whom I deal act voluntarily and, perhaps, expect a profit too. The answer is obvious; they would not act at all if they knew my circumstances, and I am taking advantage of their ignorance to risk their property. I should not like another man to do so to me, and this book teaches me, therefore, that it is wrong in me to do so to him.

Christianity requires the exercise of love and kindness in commerce.

" Scarcely for a righteous man will one die, yet peradventure for *a good man* some would even dare to die." A man may be just, and yet a monster of inhumanity. I know the common understanding is, that commerce is simply a matter of equity, and that it has no claim beyond the doing of what is just; or, rather, that it is a matter of self-interest, and has no claim beyond the doing of what is profitable. If anything else be suggested, the apt reply is, "Business is business, and charity is charity." A more erroneous maxim, a maxim more destitute of the spirit of Christianity, I have never listened to. And yet many who talk most loudly about bringing Christianity into business, talk most loudly also against bringing charity into business. And is not Christianity charity? Is it not emphatically the religion of love? And is it meant—is it possible—that the Christian spirit of love should be confined to some departments only of human life, and that it should be excluded from others? I can understand worldly men so thinking; but Christianity is designed to create a higher morality than that of the world. "What do ye more than others?" is the inquiry it addresses to its disciples,—and this inquiry may respect the common practices of even equitable trade.

It may be good political economy to "buy in the cheapest market, and sell in the dearest," but if the maxim be taken without exception and qualification, it is a great moral heresy. It may be, that my brother is unable to get by his industry enough to obtain the necessaries of life. May I take advantage of his poverty? It may be, that a tradesman is underselling his neighbours and cheating his creditors. May I patronize him? It may be, that the things I purchase are obtained at the cost of the health and life of their producers. May I innocently sanction the system, knowing its existence? I know all that is said about the laws which govern the value of labour; but I know also, that what is good law may be bad gospel, I know that man is more than a machine, I know that nothing is more unchristian than to take advantage of weakness, I know that if the value of labour were not raised artificially by our system of poor-rates (which, by the way, are contrary to all sound political economy) a very different state of things would exist. Competition may be a very good and necessary thing; but, there are a thousand cases in which mere self-interest must give place to kindness, and the Christian is the man who is bound to display the higher law of love where others think only of the law of need.

Kindness will dictate much in the carrying on of commerce which law cannot take cognizance of. It will preserve from the wretched practice of exclusive dealing—of punishing a man for his religion or politics by withholding business—of making commerce the instrument of bigotry and exclusiveness, a practice which all condemn when they suffer from it, and all approve when they are advantaged by it. And it will teach us to give a tender consideration to the cases of others, —to "be of the same mind one towards another," —to treat inferiors with courtesy and gentleness,— to pay special respect to those whose circumstances may make them most apt to suspect unkindness,— not to make a rigorous exaction of mere rights,— to allow for the operation of unavoidable causes,— and, by studious care, to smooth the path of honest poverty. "Say not unto thy neighbour, Go, and come again, and to-morrow I will give; when thou hast it by thee."

Christianity requires that a man should preserve his soul in peace and patience in commerce.

Commerce, we have said, necessarily implies

contact with others, and contact of the directest
and most interesting kind. It brings us into their
presence, and compels their intercourse. We have
to do with men under the influence of various
powerful passions, with men of different dispositions, with men of opposite principles, with men
in connection with matters of the nicest delicacy.
He who has much to do with men in any way
will be often sorely tried; but he who has much
to do with them in a way of business will be
exposed to innumerable disappointments and vexa-
tions and annoyances. He will see and feel human
nature in its most offensive and irritating forms;
he will see and feel it in its falseness, its mean
cunning, its besotted selfishness, its unfeeling harsh-
ness, its cupidity, its suspiciousness; and he will
see and feel it to his own loss and wrong. He
will be deceived by those he trusted,—injured by
those he benefited,—and, thus, in addition to the
necessary accidents of trade, have to mourn the
violation of moral integrity and the infliction of unmerited suffering. Now, it is in the enduring of all
this in meekness, the bearing of it patiently, the preserving the mind and the heart calm and unruffled
in the midst of it all, the not being provoked into
a forgetfulness of the Christian temper, the not

seeking revenge and retaliation, and the cherishing of a spirit of love and mercy for the evil and injurious, it is in this that "the power of godli-- ness" may be, and should be, displayed. It is a fine sphere for the noble principles of Christianity, sustaining, regulating, soothing the soul— a fine opportunity for revealing the dignity which belongs to the child of God and follower of Christ.— And if we are called to rise superior to the greatest troubles of life, what can be said of him who falls before its petty irritations? If we are called to endure patiently the worst inflictions of wicked men, what can be said of him whose temper fails him amid the most trifling mishaps and inconveniences?

Christianity requires *that the spirit of commerce should be checked and baptized with the spirit of holiness.*

There is, doubtless, a hardening and corrupting tendency in commercial pursuits. The constant calculation of profit and loss, the incessant contemplation of pecuniary interests, is apt to contract and debase the soul. However we explain it, the man who gives himself to the mere acquisition of gain becomes earthly, sensual, and devilish. All spiritual, noble, generous sensibilities and

F

aspirations are utterly destroyed in him. He
becomes less malleable than the coin with which
he deals. It is always dangerous to be largely
conversant with objects of self-interest, especially
in the form of money. And when the idea and
desire have got to be entertained, and the opportunity is presented, of amassing great wealth ; when
the purpose of being rich has entered the soul,
and the way to it is before the eye ; the influence
and the habit required for preservation are of no
common strength. But Christianity comes in
here to our assistance. In its light, the purely
commercial spirit is seen to be a mean, low, and
unworthy thing. It teaches that commerce is a
means, not an end,—that we are not on earth
to add field to field and house to house,—that " a
man's life consisteth not in the abundance of the
things which he possesses,"—that we may be poor,
yet having all things, and rich, yet having nothing,—that commerce is more for what it shows
than for what it gets,—that we may fail in it worst
when we succeed in it best, and succeed best when
we fail worst. Then will commerce be really
noble, be raised from the dust and clothed with
beautiful garments, become a thing not of earth
so much as of heaven, when the higher faculties

are cultivated along with the prosecution of secular pursuits, wealth is possessed and used in the spirit of stewardship, our " affections are set on things above," though our life and labours are below, and a vigorous habit of Christian liberality finds a constant vent for the acquisitions of Christian industry, and covetousness is kept in check by charity.

II. Having described, at so great a length, what a Christian should be in commerce, but little time is left *for showing why he should be it*. But this must not be omitted altogether.

Of course, all the considerations by which religion and morality are commended and enforced, are applicable here. The course, the spirit, we have pointed out is right in itself. It is what we owe to God. It is connected with eternal destiny. It is necessary to the inheritance of the kingdom of heaven. It is presented to us in the example of Christ, whom all his disciples are called to imitate. It is a dictate of that love which we can but feel if we have received his atonement. In one word— Christianity requires it. All its precepts, all its principles, all its blessings, all its prospects, require it.

But, not to dwell on these general considerations, let me adduce some particular ones.

Commerce is a most important part of our life.

It enters largely into our engagements. All have something to do with it, and many have much. It is, in some form or other, the greatest part of the life of multitudes. To exclude Christianity from it is to exclude Christianity from our largest sphere. Could it be done,—could a man be a Christian, and yet not be a Christian in his dealings with his fellows,—were it possible to retain the spirit of the Gospel, and yet not bring it into business,—what a disastrous influence would it have—how evil its action on his soul? But it is not possible. I go further. The real power of religion in our hearts must be best displayed here ; the truest test of a man's spirituality is in his secular life. It is not when we are intentionally and exclusively engaged with divine things,—it is not when, without hinderance, we seek their fellowship,—it is not when "we gird up our loins" for religious exercises,—that we give the most faithful expression to the real energy of the divine life—but, when we are about other things,—when we are off our guard,—when religion has to act spontaneously if it act at all,—when it is brought into contact

with other natures,—and when it has to oppose
the adverse influences of the world. It is often
said, "A man is really what he is relatively." I
would add, A man is spiritually what he is
secularly.

Commerce is a most influential part of our life.

It is, as I said in the first lecture, that part of
our life with which men have most to do, and of
which they can best judge. It is the world-side of
our religion. It is a necessary human operation
of our religion. Ungodly men cannot see us believe, cannot hear us pray, but they behold our
behaviour towards our brethren. And though they
may be strangers to the claims of evangelic spirituality, and utterly ignorant of doctrinal theology,
they are generally no bad critics of moral conduct.
If conscience be feeble in them, it is helped by instinct. Men have a wonderful faculty of recogniz-
ing right when it conduces to their advantage.
What, then, is our influence, if we are not holy in
business? What the use of saying, "I know the
truth," if it can be replied, "You do a lie"? Of
saying, "My conversation is in heaven," if it can
be answered, "The deeds we see are earthly and
devilish"? It must be added, that the world is
deeply interested in your commercial life. The

goodness or evil there displayed comes home to their "business and bosoms." It is not a sight, but a power, reaching and penetrating them in their tenderest part—moving their deepest feelings. For a Christian to wrong a sinner is to bring all his self-interest into active play against the Gospel. Oh! what an agency in the conversion of the world would be a blameless secular life throughout the church! It would be better than an army of ten thousand missionaries.

Commercial holiness is imperatively required by the character and temper of the times.

It is a commercial country, and age, in which we live—and commercial sinfulness is a prevailing feature. It is the duty of the Christian to adapt his example and display the virtue most wanted. Never was it more necessary for saints to "condemn the world" by secular integrity, to give a nobler example for it to follow, to bring a spirit from above to bear on its pursuits. May we be able to say, "So did not I, because of the fear of God"!

IV.

The Christian Prospering in Business.

"I spake unto thee in thy prosperity; but thou saidst,
I will not hear."

Our subject, to-night, is, "The Christian prospering in business." And, though some may think
that it concerns but a small portion of this audi-
ence, it really concerns all. Some, perhaps many
are prospering now. To them God speaks. May
they not say, "We will not hear." Some, who
are not prospering, *have prospered.* It may be
useful for them to review the past in the light of
truth,—seeing we have not done with it, when it
is done; sins, errors, faults, may be recalled and
impressed; and, what is more, the present influence
of past sins may be checked, for the faults of
prosperity remain often after prosperity has van-
ished, and it is something to rebuke what we are
after such a state, by seeing what we should have
been in it. But there is another class, perhaps the
more numerous, including most of the sanguine,
and nearly all the young, who *expect prosperity,*

and surely it may do them good in its pursuit to
feel its duties and dangers, and fit them for either
the fulfilment of their hopes, or their disappointment. So that, what with experience, memory,
and hope, I speak to all.

It certainly will not be my endeavour to define
prosperity. It would be hopeless to attempt to
satisfy you all as to what it is. "Enough" has
been described as "a little more than a man has."
And as he may be said to prosper who has
enough, and he only, I suppose that no one would
be willing, on this principle, to admit that he is
a prosperous man. There is a strange indispo-
sition to make this admission, and yet not strange.
With some it is natural; they are morbid murmurers. The times are always bad, business is
always slack. The wonder is, considering the
incessancy of their complaints, that they have
managed to live at all. It does them great credit
to get on so well in such constantly adverse circumstances. Some are backward to admit prosperity because of a conscious or an unconscious
sense of the consequences. They shrewdly suspect
the inference. They would rather not be thought
prosperous, because of human expectations and
demands; rather not think themselves so, because

of obligations and responsibilities which they know would follow. Just as a man who wishes not to be a soldier, but can only escape through disqualification, maims himself, or does his very best to bring himself under the standard height,—or as a man who would fain escape the income-tax, and is not very scrupulous, has recourse to all kinds of ingenious arts to prove that he has received less than he has. Then, there are those who manage to shield themselves by always outstripping their means. As a fact, they have not more than they want; yea, they have less. And as their expenses increase with their gains, they are always in difficulties, more or less. But this arises, not from their having little, but their spending more. He is always poor who spends more than he gets. But if we make ourselves poor by extravagant habits, we do not destroy the fact of prosperity, so far as its spiritual claims are concerned. We may fail to satisfy them, but they remain nevertheless.—Let us all remember that if we deceive ourselves and others, we cannot deceive God. He knows what he gives us, and he will require an account, not according to our own estimates or those of our brethren, but according to the real facts of the case.

It will be my endeavour, in this lecture, to point out the specific relations of Christianity to prosperity; not to show what a Christian should be, but what a prosperous Christian should be. And even with this limited object in view, I can hope only to suggest and not describe the kind of influence which Christianity should exert, without giving its reasons and instances. What does God speak to the prosperous, which they are in danger of not hearing?

I. *The voice of God to the Prosperous, which they are in danger of not hearing, concerns* HUMILITY.

This humility will be shown towards God.

There is a natural tendency in wealth to foster a spirit of sinful self-sufficience and independence of God. It is described as " sacrificing unto their net, and burning incense unto their drag; because by them their portion is fat, and their meat plenteous." It is the evil which the Jews were warned against, "Lest thou say in thine heart, my power and the might of mine hand hath gotten me this wealth." It is the danger against which Timothy was to charge the rich, "Charge them that are rich in this world, that they be not high-minded, nor trust in uncertain riches, but in the living

God, who giveth us richly all things to enjoy."
Many things conspire to this. Wealth is power.
It commands. It places at our disposal the products of nature, and the services of men. There is
nothing that may not be bought. Not only the
labour of the hands, but the thoughts, the will,
and consciences (alas!) of men may be bought.
Wealth not only gives a sort of independence, but
a sort of sovereignty. And, thus, it is an object of
esteem and reverence. "Men will praise thee
when thou doest well for thyself." "The poor
man's wisdom is despised, and his words are not
heard." And in a country where the money-
power is so strong as in ours, the possessors of
it will naturally attract a large amount of honour,
and the aristocracy of wealth will be in danger
of becoming far more conceited and supercilious
than the aristocracy of rank. Then, riches are
often associated, more or less, with industry and
skill. They are the result, in many cases, of the
application of a man's own powers. He feels that,
in a sense, he makes them. And for all these
reasons, added to the native corruption of our
hearts, it is but too likely that the rich man will
forget his entire dependence upon God.

Now, whatever natural religion may teach us,

it is certain that the Bible teaches that "God
giveth power to get wealth," and that we have
nothing "which we have not received." In many
cases, it is obviously not our virtue or ability that
has acquired our wealth. It has come to us. We
were born to an inheritance, or a good business,
or a good connection, and very little has sufficed
to preserve the advantages of our lot. But even
if not so, let our acquisitions be ever so closely
connected with our talent and labour; let us
have "created," in the fullest possible sense, our
wealth; let it be the produce of some cunning
invention, or of unremitting toil; still, who bestowed the necessary powers upon us—the sound-
ness and sagacity of mind, the vigour and health
of body? Who has preserved them? The truth
is, that our indebtedness to God is increased by
the connection between our prosperity and our
powers. Instead of lessening our obligation to
him, it is augmented by the fact that God has
not only prospered us, but also endowed us with
talent and ability to labour, and made the blessed
healthful exercise of these the means of our success. His goodness has been more delicate, his
mercy more tender. And, further, as "the race
is not to the swift, nor the battle to the strong,

nor yet riches to men of understanding," we are bound to recognize God's hand in favouring the fulfilment of our plans, and giving efficacy to our endeavours.

Now, how comprehensive is the claim for humility involved in all this? It makes every difference whether we are the authors of our wealth, or whether it is the gift of God. The largest acquisition affords not a shadow of reason for self-sufficience. Our dependence is unaffected as a fact, but it is increased, not diminished in degree. If we receive all, the more we have, the more we have received. The prosperous Christian should realize this,—and realizing this, he will be *grateful*. The bounty of Providence will endear the thought of God. In proportion to his joy will be his thankfulness.

This feeling of dependence will respect *his future* —his mode of regarding the continuance of his good things. Enough, one would think, is taught us, by constant experience, of the instability of worldly possessions. That "riches make to themselves wings and fly away," is the lesson of daily life. But it is a lesson not learned. "In my prosperity, I said, I shall never be moved," "I said, I shall one day die in my nest," is the language of men,

notwithstanding all the mutations of life. But he
who feels deeply that he is in the hands of God;
that he is in a state of probation; that the great
purpose of God is to try us, to reveal us, to exercise us, and especially to sanctify us; that we
deserve nothing, while we receive everything; and
that crosses and afflictions are often among the
most gracious methods of divine discipline; will
have a reason and a means of keeping his soul
alive to the uncertain nature of earthly property.
And if he feel not the fact more than others,
he will feel it otherwise. What with them is
merely a fact will be to him a fact full of moral
meaning. He will regard the fluctuations of life
as divine dispensations. He will not say only,
"It is the course of things," "It is the lot of
man," "It must be expected," "It can't be
helped," but he will say also, "It is the will
of God." What, therefore, others avoid, he will
entertain—what they regard as a thing that may
be, he will regard as a thing that, perhaps, ought
to be—and, while they contemplate the possibili-
ties of Providence with levity, insensibilty, or
wrath, he will contemplate them with a feeling
of dependence on a wisdom that cannot err,
and a love which is often most powerful when

most severe. He will hold his mercies with the hand of one who is not left to the caprice of chance or the despotism of fate; but who is ruled and disciplined by a providence whose forms may often change, but whose principles are always good.

Another aspect of this humility will be towards men.

"The rich answereth roughly." It is power corrupting ·the heart. No men are incapable of being injuriously affected by its possession. And, here, there is commonly a great mistake. The insolence, and tyranny, and oppression, and haughtiness of the rich are spoken of as if they were the peculiar characteristics of the favoured few. But they are really the natural results of power acting on our fallen nature. They who most cry out against the vices of the wealthy would fall into them, if they were wealthy. A transfer of riches, could it be brought about, would do no good. It would only be a transfer of the faults which they create and foster. In pleading for humility in the rich Christian, I do not advocate an impossible equality, or a forgetfulness of outward distinctions. But I mean, that the feeling of human brotherhood and of Christian respect and

G

affection should be displayed towards all; that we should "honour all men;" that we should "be of the same mind one toward another;" that we should be "courteous;" that we should feel that man is infinitely more than a bank or a railway, that the being is infinitely more than the having, that in every one we see, albeit in rags and wretchedness, and guilt, there is a real child of God, a possible heir of heaven; and that the favours of providence should only bind us to a more careful regard to the will of our common father, and a more delicate respect to the feelings of our brethren. The pride of prosperity is seen offensively when a man gets above his companions, outgrows the familiars of his early life, knows not his once chosen associates and bosom friends. It is seen more offensively when he denies or ignores his kindred, recognizes not his own house, ashamed of his parents, the father by whose industry he was nourished, the mother who watched over and comforted his childhood and his youth. And it is seen most offensively of all when he despises the poor saints of the Most High, shuns the righteous with whom he once delighted to commune and pray, withdraws from the humble church to which, perhaps, he owes both worlds, and leaves the excellent of the earth for the society of the gay and gorgeous.

II. *The voice of God to the prosperous, which they are in danger of neglecting, respects* SPIRITUALITY.

Extravagance, worldliness, and indolence are the frequent accompaniments of the state we speak of. Let it not, however, be supposed that we mean to condemn the enjoyment of worldly good. We know of nothing in reason or Scripture which makes it wrong for a man to make use of the means given him by God for increasing the comforts and delights which appeal to sense and soul. We have not learned that privation is piety, and wretchedness virtue. We are to " rejoice in our portion," and, if through a gracious providence, we can command a larger measure than many of the gratifications and graces of life, it is no dishonour to that providence to surround ourselves with the ministries of physical, and social, and artistic good, thus cultivating and gladdening the tastes which the God of beauty and of love has implanted in our nature. Nor do we thus, of necessity, deprive our brethren of what is theirs,—nor of what might be better used for them. Multitudes live by the things which are not

indispensable to human existence, and he who
spends money on luxuries may be distributing that
money in the best and most effectual manner. We
are not enemies to enjoyment. We do, indeed,
honour the man who makes a sacrifice of his all for
the comfort and salvation of his brethren, who
living on the simplest fare devotes himself wholly
to men. There have been those—and they are
worthy—who, foregoing pleasures most sweet and
high and refined pursuits, have humbled and im-
poverished themselves from the noblest of all
motives, the love of Christ and souls. But they are
not the necessary models of the saints. This is not
given to all. The evil thing about many is that
they do not truly enjoy their prosperity,—that they
have not the conditions which are essential to
it,—that they abridge their happiness by the very
measures they take to secure it. It may easily appear that Christianity by preserving spirituality
really preserves happiness.

Spirituality is opposed to *extravagance*.

" Let your moderation be known unto all men."
It was a reproach of the Jews that " according to
their pasture, so were they filled." And the
temptation of prosperity is for a man to multiply
his expenses simply because he can meet them,—

to enlarge the sphere and heighten the style of his life in accordance with his power,—and thus to become a prey to luxury. Luxury has almost always attended wealth. In the case of nations, it has caused decay and destruction by weakening and debasing and corrupting the people. And so in the case of individuals, it is fatal to lofty principle and noble habits, the vigour and health of intellect and heart, conscience and will. I cannot tell the point at which the sinfulness of indulgence begins. It may be a shifting one. But he who prizes the manliness and integrity of his soul—he who would not render himself unfit for the possible reverses of life—he who would maintain a taste for the most exalted pleasures—he who is duly alive to the perilous corruption within him, ever ready like a magazine of powder to ignite from the smallest spark, or like a river, on the removal of a little portion of embankment, to burst forth with desolating violence—he will rather err on the side of defect than excess, and "deny himself" too much than smooth the way and strengthen the temptations of "the lust of the eye, the lust of the flesh, and the pride of life." He will beware how he enervates himself by disproportionate gratification—he will beware how by artificial wants and

habits he makes necessary to himself and those
with whom he has to do a state which cannot be
secured—he will beware how he enters on a race
of rivalry with the better or as well to do around
him—he will beware how he pampers the flesh,
and gives undue growth to the lower passions of
his soul, while the nourishment of the higher with
the things of God is neglected.

Spirituality is opposed to *worldliness.*

This may be where there is no extravagance, no
luxury. I need not repeat what I have before
said as to the secularizing tendency of commerce.
Prosperity is closely allied to secularity. It generally supposes much engagement in secular things,
and occasions more,—it brings into the fellowship
of secular men,—and it augments secular fears
and hopes and joys. Hence secularity—worldliness—the inordinate occupation of the mind with
what is present, "things seen." Worldliness is a
common growth of prosperity. Multitudes who
are not luxurious are worldly. They may shun
society, they may be misers and misanthropes,
they may have no taste for elegant display and
no propensity to sensual vices, and yet be worldly.
If asked to describe worldliness, so fatal to the
prosperous, I should say that it is the want of

spiritual sympathy, spiritual perception, spiritual taste, spiritual power. It is that state in which a man would be if he had no divine capabilities, if his religious faculties were extracted. It may or may not be associated with physical lusts, love of money, fondness for show. He is worldly who "walks" not "with God," whose "conversation is" not "in heaven," whose "affections are" not "set on things above," who has no keen eye for the mysteries of the kingdom, no quick ear for its voices, no delicate sensibility to its impressions. Have you not many before your minds who have become worldly through prosperity? You cannot say they have become brutes or knaves. On the contrary, the moralities may be all maintained, the forms of religion may be all observed, but the glory has departed, it is habit not life, the remains of former faith not the effects of present faith. The freshness, the vigour, the brightness are no more; the gush of feeling is no more; the trembling at God's word, the peace and joy in believing, the "Speak, Lord, for thy servant heareth," the lively hope, the agonizing prayer, are no more. They are worldly. A thick crust of secularity has formed around the souls once instinct and tender with holy vitality.

Spirituality is opposed to *indolence*.

Prosperity says, "Take thine ease," and men are but too ready to comply with the suggestion. Fulness is unfavourable to activity. Hence it happens that as men get on in the world, they gradually become indisposed for the services to which they were devoted in days of poverty and humbleness. Or else manifold toils and anxieties exhaust both strength and spirit, and the hours not given to business are required to recruit the wearied energies, which are capable of no more elaborate exploit on week evenings than desultory conversation and light reading, no more disinterested service on Sabbath days than attendance on services which must not exercise but only soothe their minds. The works in which they were used to be active are left to others—the school, the houses of wretchedness and ignorance, see them no more. And prosperity, while it causes this decline, helps to cover it. The man well-to-do contributes to societies that perform the works in which he was engaged. He works by proxy. He assigns his sphere to others. He is not idle. He supports all good things. But, my brother, the power to do this is additional to those you used to have—not instead of them. You did good then by personal service. That obligation remains. The ability to give does not destroy the ability to labour, and the purse cannot answer the demand for activity and effort.

It is a sad thing that the prosperous are so often the spiritually idle—taking their ease in Zion. The world needs the work as well as the wealth of Christians—but alas! work and wealth are often both withheld. And is it not for a lamentation, in this view, that the rich are so generally retiring from the scenes of their business, seeking recreation and repose in suburban residences, and giving their example and influence where they are least needed? What is to become of the millions of our great city, I fear to think, if the wealthy abandon them, and devote to scattered populations what is so greatly needed by dense masses of souls.

III. *The Voice of God to the prosperous, which they are in danger of neglecting, regards* BENEVOLENCE.

The design of God, in blessing is to make us blessings, and if He have largely endowed us with worldly good, it is that we may minister to others. Indeed, none are exempt. The blessedness of giving, so much greater than that of receiving, is not confined to a few. All may enjoy it, and He who noticed the widow's mite will estimate our gifts, if we be poor, according to our poverty, as well as, if we be rich, according to our riches. Yea, they that cannot give need not be deprived of this luxury—they may get the power—"working," as Paul says, "that they may have to give." And if God have prospered us, so that we have more than we require for ourselves—do we not hear him say, "Be rich in good works, ready to distribute, willing to communicate?" The very means of riches, the common way and method of getting rich, should teach this lesson. Why has God appointed commerce? Why made it necessary? Why given to men different faculties and spheres? Why made them dependent on each other? Is it not all designed to impress the doctrine of brotherhood, and to draw out affections and promote deeds in keeping with it? Does it not say, "No man can live of himself, all serve one another of necessity, there is mutual indebtedness, therefore do good, by love serve one another, be ready to every good work"? And when we look at the Gospel, is not this truth and duty made solemn and tender beyond all the thoughts of men? Do we not there see that we are *stewards*—stewards of God—and that for the

poor, the wretched, the lost? Do we not there see
that to "occupy" till Christ comes is the nature
and term of our possession? Do we not there see
that immense importance will be attached in the day
of judgment to the manner of our occupation—to
our mode of using property? Do we not there see
that charity to souls and bodies will be one of the
chief tests of character, and conditions of recompense? Do we not there meet with the argument
for liberality derived from Christ's being rich and
becoming poor to make us rich? Are we not there
taught that to love and minister are the essential
principle and service of the Gospel—and that without them we cannot know God's grace, nor do
God's will, in giving us prosperity?

The prosperous Christian should be a liberal
Christian. It is not enough that he continue his
gifts—he must increase them. Proportion is God's
rule. He estimates what we part with according
to what we keep. Alas! many give not more but
less as the means of giving are augmented. The
temptation of prosperity is selfishness. The desire
to amass is strengthened by gain. Acquisitiveness
grows like other passions, by exercise. The love
of money is fed by money. The opportunity and
power of accumulation draw out the disposition to

accumulate. Many who care not to be rich, while they are poor, become anxious to be so when a beginning has been made, and success proves as a little water down a dry pump. The thought is suggested, the wish is excited, by the possession of the means. Then, also, the prosperous are apt to be removed from the pressing claims of sorrow and need. They get out of the way of distress. And this is one reason why the poor are often the kindest to the poor. Others know less of the poor, and are tempted to think, amidst their own sufficiency, that their brethren must be better off than they are. So it comes to pass that men often keep up no proportion between their acquisitions and their gifts. The poor and middle-classes give, as a rule, far more than the wealthy, as all our charitable and religious societies can testify—give far more, that is, in proportion to their means.

But so it should not be. And if religion were a vigorous principle, so it would not be. A healthy saint will delight in being able to relieve his brethren, and one of the chief charms of prosperity will be the power it gives him to be a minister for good. His first care will be "his own"—the needy kindred whose trials he may soothe by generous gifts, or whom he may more worthily and wisely serve by enabling them to serve themselves. His next will be the welfare of those by whose assistance he has succeeded. He will not think his duty done by a mere payment of wages— by giving only what he is obliged to give and they to take, but he will feel that their claim on him, as a Christian, is much larger, and by manifold kind devices he will seek to promote their physical and mental and moral well-being. And beyond these he will look to the world, " doing good to all, especially to those who are of the household of faith," rejoicing in being permitted to comfort and assist the members of Christ's body. And when he looks to those that are " without," he will mainly care that they may be saved—saved through " the belief of the truth " which he possesses and can dispense—not however forgetting that they " are in the flesh," nor failing to imitate his example who fed the body while he taught the soul. He will not waste his money by thoughtless distribution, nor think it enough that he dispenses, but be " wise to do well," and, as selection is inevitable, he will do most of that which is most needed, always " devising liberal things, and by liberal things shall he stand."

V.

The Christian Failing in Business.

"If thou faint in the day of adversity, thy strength
is small."

WE have to consider the Christian failing in
business. It is not a pleasant subject, but it is a
necessary one. There are such failures, and they
are sufficiently connected with the welfare and
influence of the saint to be made the subject of
illustration by the light of the Gospel. Christianity does not secure its disciples against misfortune and calamity. It is not a violation of the
laws of nature and of mind,—it does not work a
constant miracle in favour of its followers,—it does
not command the "sun and moon" to stand still
while they achieve their secular exploits. It came
to "fulfil, not destroy" the law—and its relation
to natural ordinances is the same as its relation to
moral rules—it consummates, not despises, gives
higher ends and motives, instead of weakening
their obligation or impeaching their character.
Further, Christianity has need of trouble. While

H

it could not help it always without a constant
miracle—it does not help it always when it can.
God has a use for affliction to his people. It is a
lesson—a discipline. It "works together" with
good.

I grant that there is a tendency in religion,
deep, enlightened, vigorous religion, to promote
worldly prosperity. It cannot be otherwise. It
is part of the universal "profitableness" of godliness, which has "the promise of the life that
now is." Most of the conditions of secular success are improved by the principles and habits of
spirituality. It quickens the intellect, it gives
calmness and self-possession to the feelings, it
fosters industry and diligence, making them a
duty, it creates character and credit. In these
and many other ways, it tends to make a prosperous man, independently of that blessing of
God upon his work which Christianity teaches
us to acknowledge, that "blessing which maketh
rich," and which, in a thousand modes, besides
the violation of fixed laws, may bring proceedings
to a profitable issue, which, without it, would,
however wisely conceived and energetically pro-
secuted, end in a disastrous failure. Many a man
may be found who has been made, in this sense,

by godliness. He owes to it literally everything. Its influence on him even here has been universal. There is no part of his being or his lot that has not been, so to speak, redeemed by Christ.

But while we maintain the tendency of religion to secular success, that tendency may not be fully developed. The Christian is not perfect, and he may hinder its development. The world is wicked, and it may obstruct it. God knows that there is often something better than prosperity for his people, and he may interfere with it. In other words, a Christian may fail through his own fault, his want of skill, of consistency, of economy, of industry,—or he may fail through the fault of others—being dependent on those less wise, and honest and active than himself, or on those who deceive and defraud him,—or he may be placed in circumstances which are adverse to his advancement, and be foiled in his best endeavours by unforeseen and unaccountable events, neither within his own nor others' control.

Some Christians never get on,—they are always a burden to themselves and others,—they try many schemes with one result. Some fall into calamity suddenly—trouble comes upon them in a moment. Some descend gradually and by many steps—entering a deepening shadow—until they have "no light." With some failure is succeeded by prosperity,—with some it is followed by a long course of struggles and toils ending at last in "a broad and wealthy place."

My subject is not, then, for those only who "fail" in the technical sense—those who are brought to a complete stand—who have to meet their creditors and proclaim their insolvency. It is more general. It applies to all to whom life is a trial as well as a toil, whose hopes are followed by sore disappointment, who know the bitterest of all fears, the fear of being unable to render to every man his due, whose spirits are burdened by the pressure of heavy losses, whose greatest fortitude is required to endure their troubles, whose severest wisdom is scarce sufficient to stave off ruin. They may not appear to the world to fail. The deepest things do not always appear at all. It is not necessarily in the court of bankruptcy that the sorest sorrow is seen. The sorrow of those is often the greatest who are struggling to keep out of it. The unrevealed distress is frequently the deepest as well as most honourable. "The heart knoweth its own bitterness."

In dealing with this subject I shall do as I have

done before, endeavour to say what is peculiar to it
and not what is common to all subjects. It is the
Christian in failure that is before us, and it will be
my study to point out the influence which his
Christianity should exert upon him in that condition. And may that God who "doeth all things"
and doeth them all "well" bless our words!

I. *Christianity should preserve from Despondency
in failure.*

There is a tendency in trouble to dispirit. I
know that it may be checked by the force of
natural energy of heart. There are some who, even
without religion, are so sanguine, so resolute, so
confident, that they feel it not, or but little. They
are buoyant and rise to the surface, however for a
time they may sink. Yea, difficulty seems to in-
spirit them. They are stimulated by opposition—
aroused by failure—as a race-horse has been known
to win the race through the excitement of being
overthrown. But these are choice souls—the
greater number are apt to sink,—and not a few are
altogether dependent on success. They cannot row
against the tide. They can do well when their
efforts tell, but they lose heart when their efforts
seem to be but a "beating of the air." They are

naturally timid, and disposed to augur evil, and their strength is gone when their work is lost. And even those who are armed and nerved by temporary calamity often yield when calamity is long continued. The daily pressure of difficulty, the constant occurrence of defeat, wear out the soul of the strongest,—and they who presented only a bold front to the foe on his first assault, become utterly exhausted by protracted engagements with him. For sorrow is stimulating only along with hope. With the prospect of rising, more vigorous efforts may be made through its pressure, but when that prospect has disappeared, the heart of the most valiant may sink within him, and his depression will be great in proportion to his former buoyancy— for they who give themselves most to grief and inactivity are often those who, up to a certain point, are most sanguine and determined.

Now the evil of this depression is great. It is great in relation to that which causes it—the worldly business. When the heart is low, the opportunity of deliverance is not seen, and the means of it are not employed. If it be felt that there is but little hope of amending the case, that there is no chance of extrication out of trouble,— or if the powers be paralyzed by humiliation and

suffering,—the very thing needed to redemption
is wanted. And hence many who fall into great
adversity remain there. They never recover the
shock. Instead of devising means of extrication,
they give themselves up to despondency, and to
indulge in idle regrets over the past instead of
making energetic efforts to repair its misfortunes.
Many a man may be found who was once the
active, sanguine, excited man of business, but who
now presents a strange contrast to his former self.
He is as one possessed with a spirit of defeat—as
one prostrated by an irresistible fate—as one who
has been stunned by a terrible collision with providence. No ingenuity to plan, no vivacious seizure
of suggested thoughts, no prompt handling of presented instruments, no vigorous employment of
offered opportunities. He waits for openings—or
seeks them in the mood in which they are sure not
to be found. And if, by chance or the agency of
others, he have the means of relief and recovery, he
uses them in a way which no means, nothing but
miracles, could bear.

But the worst of this despondency is that it
affects other things. Begun in business, it extends
to all departments of feeling and activity. The
whole tone of being is lowered. The general

interest is depressed. The spirit is like a broken bow. ' The slackened gait, the careless habit, the sleepy thought, the irresolute will, all betoken the sad change that has passed upon the man. Yea, morals and religion are not exempted. The social relation is treated as all else. Languor has seized benevolence, and even integrity. There is no heart any more for doing good. "The house" is no longer "a church." It is easy to perceive that his religion has declined. He has lost its earnestness, if not its vital principle. How many are now, as to godliness, the mere wrecks of their former selves, whose decline may be traced to adversity! Mortification, indifference, distrust of God, have eaten out the core of all holy affection— and their fall into trouble was the beginning of their fall into utter irreligion.

Now, how does Christianity tend to check this evil tendency? It limits *the sphere of failure,*—it teaches that secular calamity is but a small part of calamity—that there are many and mightier mischiefs. In its light, the world itself is but a small, brief, poor thing. It takes worldly fortunes out of all the regions which it behoves a man most to care for and to cultivate. It says that the greatest bankruptcy is not of fortune but of faith—that the

worst bargain may be that by which "the whole
world" is gained. It opens a prospect compared
with which this life is but a moment. And it ad-
monishes us not to estimate ourselves by our affairs
but our affairs by ourselves. What a stay is this
against despondency, if it be realized. If it be
realized that I may succeed as a spirit, and for
eternity, though I should fail in every earthly pro-
ject,—that God may give me a portion transcend-
ing all thought, while he withholds every worldly
good,—that I may be more precious to him in want
and woe than they that have "all things richly to
enjoy,"—will it not perfect strength in me?

But if Christianity limit the sphere of failure, it
also *changes its character.* It teaches us that if
we fail, it may be a means of our greater success.
The prostration, the sorrow, the want may be the
discipline of life everlasting. By them the heart
may be made better, faith and love and patience
may be proved and perfected, character matured
for heaven, holy principle invigorated and chastened
for usefulness. Thus regarding earthly failure, instead of despondency, it may produce elation, and
"joy in tribulation" become the high and mysterious attainment of the saint. For he sees God
not fighting against him but for him,—his strongest

love is revealed in his being able to chasten him,—providence is not covered with "clouds and darkness," but shines brightly even on his tears,—the "inward man is renewed" while "the outward man perishes,"—and he drinks the cup of woe, even while conscious of its distastefulness, with a cheerful temper, as the medicine of life.

Nor are these considerations inapplicable in cases where failure may be directly traced to the Christian's own fault—where he can plainly see that had he been wiser, more industrious, or even more honourable, it would not have taken place. There is providence even then. God is not to be excluded. Because he works according to a settled system, we may not deny his work. And even then is he gracious. The trouble is not less a paternal chastisement, because it comes immediately from our filial fault. We should see the chastisement more distinctly for that—feel it more painfully. It is not a general but a particular discipline. It calls not only for improvement, but for penitence. It does not say, God is against us, but only against our sin and folly—and it aims not at our destruction but our salvation. Instead of giving ourselves up to despair, we should hear the voice which summons us to consideration and amendment—and thus

failure may be our success. We may rise by falling.
And even rise in the same sense as that in which
we fall. We may have a better prospect of prosperity than ever. For God only withholds worldly
good for the soul's greater profit—and, therefore,
without estimating men's spiritual state by their
secular, it may be that sorrow having done its work,
joy may take its place. If not, still a better joy.

II. *Christianity should preserve from Irritation
in failure.*

If the timid are most in danger of despondency,
the proud are most in danger of exasperation.
And who is so free from pride as to be in no
danger hence? It is annoying to have one's
schemes fail,—it is annoying to be placed in a
position of inferiority, and especially to descend to
it from a higher,—it is annoying to be deprived of
accustomed enjoyments and powers,—it is annoying to be an object of blame, perhaps more so to
be an object of pity. Therefore failure may easily
excite the evil passions of the soul—may sour
the temper—may arouse to anger and to wrath.
And if a man cannot easily brook restraint, if
he have a high opinion of his own cleverness
and power, if he have made it a grand object

to stand well and high in the world, and especially if he have been honourably anxious to maintain a good repute for integrity—it is certain that one of the chief operations of religious principle will be to soothe his perturbed heart, to calm his irritated temper.

If a man were only irritated against himself— if he were aroused only to severe self-rebuke and complaint, it might not be amiss. Indeed, the design of religion is to promote this self-condemnation, and to enable us to discover its fit occasions. We can be seldom wrong in severely judging ourselves. The danger is the other way. But we may be very wrong, and often are, in judging of others. We read of "charging God foolishly"—and it is by no means an uncommon thing for men to indulge their anger at the expense of divine dispensations. Propriety may dictate silence—though it does not always secure it. The rash speech occasionally indicates a passion which cannot be restrained. But where there is no speech, there may be rebellious feeling—feeling, which, if it dare, would arraign the wisdom, the benevolence, and even the equity of divine procedure.—But we are most at fault in reference to *men*. And, owing to the connection between us and others, the close fellowships of secular society, the necessary dependence of commerce on intercourse and interchange, it is seldom that an opportunity is not afforded for the exercise of a querulous and revengeful spirit towards men. The failing man is therefore often found cherishing a wrong temper towards his fellows. Friends have not done what they might and should,—parties have not given the support and encouragement within their power,—agents and partners have been wanting in befitting qualities. But the greatest occasion of an unchristian spirit is where failure has been produced by the blameworthy conduct of others— where promises have been broken on which the fullest dependence was placed—where representations have been falsified on which action was taken —where confidence has been betrayed by falsehood and dishonesty. These are irritating cases. It is hard to " love our enemies " at all times—but it is especially hard in cases of ruinous fraud. I question if it be not easier to love our persecutors, than to love those who ruin us by deceit and wrong. Persecution is not so personal a thing. It is aimed chiefly at Christ,—we feel that he is wronged in us,—we have " the fellowship of his sufferings." But, in the other case, the evil comes home most to ourselves,—we are its subjects and its objects,—we are not so directly the representatives of a greater being and a greater claim, —and we are *taken in* as well as injured.

Now what does Christianity, what should it do, to soothe this irritability of failure? "It lays the axe to the root." Irritation comes mainly from pride—that pride it mortifies. It begets *humility*. Is not the first lesson of its knowledge that we are "*fools*"—the first lesson of its holiness that we are *sinners?* Does it not exalt by abasing us— strengthen by weakening us? Are we tempted to impeach *God?* Its language is, What is thy finite judgment against infinite intelligence? What is thy passionate verdict of interest and feeling against the calm eternal thought? What is thy opposition to the supremacy of God? What is thy complaint of evil, who hast sinned away every favour, and livest only upon grace? Are we tempted to wrath against *men?* Its language is, Thou hast more wronged God than any men have wronged thee. The very wickedness that arouses thy anger thou hast been guilty of in a higher sphere, and against an infinitely more glorious being.

And if it produces humility, it produces *bene-*

volence—love kindled at the cross, fed by the
matchless kindness of our God and Saviour—
kindness shown to us as enemies, and treating
us with delicacy and tenderness as well as be-
stowing upon us bounty. We are taught "to
love our enemies"—our directest and most mali-
cious foes. And if we do, we shall see in this
very sin against ourselves an argument for compassion. Our thought will be, "Oh! how they
wrong themselves,—they injure our substance, but
they far more terribly. injure their own souls,—
they damage our temporal interests, but they ruin
their immortal nature,"—and our resentment will
be lost in our commiseration.—And even in the
case of most manifest human wrong, we shall be
able to rise above human agency. For Christianity instructs us that even the wicked are God's
"hand." We may not exclude him when we can
include others—for there is a wisdom that over-
rides human plans and a power that overrules
human actions. The wicked should be more to
us than the wicked, — they should be to us the
instruments of providence,—and we should hear
a voice, amidst the greatest din of human sounds
saying, "Be still and know that I am God."

III. *Christianity should preserve from Dishonesty in failure.*

Want is a temptation to dishonesty. I do not say it is an excuse for it. I am about to say the very reverse. But it is a temptation to it. It is a great trial when a man does not possess the means of obtaining that which he has been wont to enjoy, a greater when he does not possess the means of obtaining that which is necessary to his subsistence, and a greater still to a generous nature when those that are dependent on him suffer with himself. "Men do not despise a thief if he steal to satisfy his soul when he is hungry." They may condemn him, and punish him, but the act is mitigated by the necessity—and compassion will modify the sentence of morality. It is said to be one of the dangers of poverty, "Lest I be poor and steal." Dishonesty is not the universal attendant on poverty, any more than pride is on wealth, but the tendency of destitution is in that direction.

Many who never had a thought that was not honourable have fallen into sin when they fell into trouble. And even when the trouble has been much less than entire failure. There are things as hard to bear as penury—yea, harder—the being known

to be poor, the losing social caste, the being
shunned by former companions, the being excluded from the once-frequented society. And,
in a country like ours, where so much stress is
laid on a man's circumstances, where "the praise"
is so loud "if thou doest well for thyself," where
success covers so much sinfulness, and the "respectability" of fortune obtains an easy excuse for
many things anything but respectable in conduct,
these evils press sorely on the fallen.

Hence the temptation to do wrong to evade
or conceal or repair misfortune. Hence the continuance of expenses after the means of meeting
them have ceased in the hope of future ability.
Hence the daring speculation, the suspending
honesty on the chances of the market. Hence
the bill, the postponing shame by pawning credit.
Hence the taking advantage of those who are
known to be too weak or too easy to assert their
rights. And hence that most common of all
wrongs, the using the protection of the law as
if it were a liquidation of the debt.

Christianity will teach us to avoid all these
and all other modes of escaping from trouble by
committing iniquity. It allows of no escape that
is not compatible with purest truth, integrity, and

I

"the doing to others as we would they should do unto us." True, it is a great trial that we should suffer want—suffer the hardships, the privations, the social excommunications, of poverty. And as a trial, it treats it. It is one of the things which we are not to think "strange," one of the disciplines we are to bear and profit by, one of the temptations we are to have fortitude to resist, one of the fields in which Christian principle is to gain a victory over the dictates of flesh and the example of the world.

If religion do anything for us, it gives us "*a good and honest heart*," it makes us right, it fills us with a deep hatred to all deceit and fraud. One of the chief troubles of a saint in failure will be the thought or fear of others being injured. It will distress him more than his own sufferings, that others should suffer through him, even if without his fault. But if he feel thus, how can he increase the sufferings of others for the sake of his own interests? To be the accidental cause of their not having their own will pain him—how can he intentionally injure or hazard their prosperity?

Making us to love truth and equity, *Christianity connects our self-respect with these principles.* A

Christian will feel that *what he is* is the great point—that character is above condition. He will say, "Poverty is no crime or shame. It cannot affect my dignity as a spirit, though it may trouble me as a body. The vicissitudes of fortune cannot touch the true manhood. I am debased only by sin." Adversity, in the Gospel light, may increase his worth and honour. It is a nobler thing to bear its searching test, than to ride in the high places of the earth. The Son of God was a poor man. Incarnate Deity had not where to lay His head.

And, as Christians, we shall be supremely concerned for the moral honour of Christianity. We shall go far, and bear much, to shield it from unmerited blame—not giving occasion to those who seek occasion. That men should be able to pervert our conduct into an impeachment of it will be a great affliction,—but that our conduct should itself impeach it—why, the thought will be worse than death.

VI.

The Christian in Temporary Retirement from Business.

"Quiet resting-places."

To speak of cessation from business—to urge retirement—to hint that the hand should be withdrawn from its handy-work—will sound, I am well aware, very strange and perhaps very ridiculous to some. "What," they may exclaim, "sacrifice opportunities of getting money? We never heard of such a thing! Is it not the main chance, the one thing needful? We are not so foolish as that. To get what we can, and keep what we get, is our motto. As for doing less than is absolutely necessary—we should regard it as a crime, yea, as what has been said to be worse than that—a blunder." But if I address any one disposed to speak in this way, I would just say to him, Has it ever occurred to you that you may so pursue business as to destroy *the power* of doing it? Let money be the chief good, but is it wise to accumulate even the chief good at the cost of losing it altogether?

Suppose thy excessive eagerness should bring on
a fit of apoplexy—should weaken or destroy thy
mind—should waste away prematurely thy vigour
of body—where would thy wisdom be? Besides,
if thou art getting the chief good, is getting all?
Is there to be no *enjoyment* of it? And no *use* of
it? Is the end attained in having? Art thou a
mere depository of wealth—an intelligent bank, a
conscious rail-way? Is that thy shrewdness and
sagacity? Is it thus thy worldly wisdom rebukes
the silliness of others? But, my brother, the gain
on which thou hast set thine heart, and which thou
thinkest it a great mistake and weakness to forego
in any measure, will not last long. I presume
that thou believest thou wilt survive it—survive
it for ever. And does it accord with reason to let
thy nature be neglected for the sake of temporary
possessions? Take your own ground—should acquisitiveness concern only a brief period of thy
being? What wouldest thou think of a man that
invested all his money in something that would be
sure to perish in a week? He would be far wiser
than thou who sacrificest thine immortality to
secular profit.

I. In speaking of those retirements which are

incumbent on the Christian in the midst of secular life, I shall omit those which are compulsory and confine myself to those which are voluntary—and shall treat of them in relation to their ends rather than their seasons.

The first end is health.

And this I put on the ground of duty. I suppose there would be no doubt as to his guilt who destroys his life, or as to his who maims his body. If a man kill himself, or if he deprive himself of some bodily organ, we pronounce him a grave offender. Why? Because he has no right to do it. He is not his own proprietor. He did not make himself, nor has he preserved himself. He owes himself to God and is responsible to him for living as long as he can and as well as he can—responsible for his existence and his powers as far as they are under his control. Now a man may kill himself by excessive toil and care just as well as by poison or the knife. The suicide may be he who cuts off his days by putting a strain on flesh and soul which they are unable to endure. Sometimes this is done knowingly. A man has before him the certainty that his course must terminate in premature death, or he might know it ; the laws of life would teach him so, if he duly considered them. And if he who maims his body is a sinner, is not he who destroys the vigour and elasticity of his powers, physical or mental? Is the destruction of an eye as great an evil as the general weakness and weariness of the whole nature?

Now there is no law more clear and indubitable than that rest is necessary to health. We were not made for unremitting toil. And if this ordinance be violated, it will tell somewhere. There may be seeming exceptions—but they are only seeming ones. There will be abridgment of existence, or paralysis of powers, or general lassitude, or morbid feeling, if mind and body be kept on an unnatural stretch of labour, and they are not recruited and invigorated by repose. And if "the life is more than meat and the body than raiment," and if life and the vigour of life are trusts from God, if the first duty is self-preservation, that duty on which all others must depend—there can be no doubt as to the obligation I am urging.

Enjoyment is another end.

We were made for happiness—various kinds of pleasurable sensation and emotion. It is quite a mistake to think that God delights in our misery. "He does not afflict willingly," and when he does

afflict, it is for the sake of our happiness. One end
of God is always our enjoyment. Benevolence
must contemplate it. Now, he who gives himself
to unremitting toil cannot enjoy the gifts of providence as it is meant he should. He may have much
pleasure in the very exercise of his faculties—but
there is a pleasure in the calm contemplation of
the divine bounty, in the unbinding and relaxation
of the soul, and in the gratification of its varied
tastes by the means afforded by success, which is
impossible to him. He feasts at God's table but
it is a hurried and an unquiet meal—he rests on
God's pillow, but it is a dreamy and disturbed slum-
ber. The season of enforced cessation of worldly
work is begrudged, and intruded upon by worldly
cares. He has no time for the peaceful flow of
happy feeling—for survey and review—for grateful expatiation—for giving free vent to natural
sensibilities. He knows not the blessedness of
stillness and silence. He lives wholly without, and
not within. Existence is a hurried movement.
He is always in a feverish excitement. He is like
one who labours only in the sun, and never seeks
the calm cool shade. The bow is kept bent till its
spring is lost. He obtains a portion, but does not
" rejoice in it." He holds property, but does not

possess it. He builds a house, but does not inhabit it. He has gorgeous apparel, but does not wear it. His connection with his lot is that of title and outward law, not of fresh and joyous interest.

The general cultivation of faculty is an end.

Business requires and sharpens some faculties—and in connection with other things it may exercise a sanitary and invigorating influence upon many faculties. But when it is pursued, as it must be by him who does nothing else, it has but a limited influence for good, and a powerful influence for evil. It is well known that the powers necessary to the greatest secular success are none of the highest, and that they may have but a small range. Acquaintance with the rules and methods of procedure, activity, sharpness, readiness, ingenuity, may suffice for a prosperous course. A man may get on well and wonderfully, and yet be grossly ignorant of almost everything but what concerns his trade or profession, and yet have no power of thought, no refinement of taste, no sympathy with the higher forms of truth and beauty and goodness, no generous impulses and aspirations. His only reading may be the "city article"—his only meditation the state of the market—his only esti-

mate, profit—his only aspiration, gain. He may
have, in high perfection, the activity, the cunning,
the quickness, the perseverance, which belong to
many portions of the animal world, and be almost
entirely destitute of the distinguishing endowments
of a rational and moral being. Now, we say, that
retirement from business should be sought in order
that the mind be furnished and expanded with
knowledge, that it be refined and elevated by
literature, that noble affections be nourished by the
study and contemplation of noble natures, that
social sympathies be developed by intercourse, and
that principles more lofty and disinterested than
those which rule the world of commerce may be
fed and fostered.

Religion is an end which needs retirement.

In the second lecture, in speaking upon this
subject, I said that devotional engagements have
the same relation to active life that food has to
exercise. It is true that religion may be seen and
cherished in our common work, and so may the
strength derived from nourishment—that is, work
may be useful to spiritual life as to physical life,
but it does not follow that either can dispense with
nutriment. The religion which dwells only in
secret is in danger of becoming a morbid, super-

stitious sentiment—as the man who eats and does not labour is in danger of disease and death—but still there must be the reception of food, and still there must be private devotion. The world is the place in which to exercise and apply spiritual principles, rather than the place in which to get or increase them—or, if exercise does strengthen, it will not do so without truth and grace to be obtained elsewhere. It is by the study of the book of life, by deep meditation on spiritual things, by intercourse with Christ, by earnest prayer, by severe self-examination, that we must minister to the principles and habits of holiness, that we must "exercise ourselves unto godliness." He who neglects the closet, or who abridges the time spent there, or who brings to its duties a jaded body and wearied soul, or who merely performs them as duties, does them as a task, will soon lose the energy by which alone the heart can be kept permanently above the world, by which alone the world can be preserved in its place of a servant and be prevented usurping that of a lord.

Benevolent activity is an end of retirement.

We may not stop at personal religion. There is a call for more than that. We live in a state in which the greatest demands are made for the holy

energies of every saint. While business is being
pursued, souls are being lost. While wealth is
being accumulated, immortal natures are perishing. Worldly affairs are attended to at the cost
of men's salvation. For can it be doubted that the
salvation of men would be largely promoted if
those Christians who give themselves wholly to
secular life were to devote a portion of their time
to good works—to intercourse with the sinful—to
earnest endeavours to teach and warn them?
Need I specify *the family?* By incessant work
how is that defrauded? No opportunity is afforded
for cultivating the confidence and affection of the
household—for instructing them in the doctrines
and duties of religion and morality—for moulding
their character by a holy and wise influence—for
setting before them the winning pattern of Christian love and noble principle. Need I mention
the school—the neighbourhood—the church—whose
wants and spheres are neglected by the over busy
saint? Inquire of one, if he will do something in
the way of useful effort, and the answer is, "I
keep such late hours, I don't get home till such a
time, I pray thee have me excused." Inquire of
another, and he replies, "Why really I am so
hard worked in the week that I am not fit for any-

thing on the Sunday, I pray thee have me
excused." Inquire of a third, and he pleads that
the influence of his secular engagements destroys
the taste and aptitude for such occupations, and
he prays to be excused. And why is all this?
Are the men struggling with poverty? Have
they the greatest difficulty to make both ends
meet? Are they threatened with insolvency? In
many instances it is so, but in many it is not, but
the reverse. This engrossment is voluntary—it is
sought. They have gone thus deeply into secular
things with their eyes open, and of their own
accord. They have steadily and purposely increased their concerns, embracing opportunities
for enlarging their business—they have more than
is needful, but have determined to have more still
—and the meaning of their conduct, rightly interpreted, is this, "We are doing so much for
ourselves that we cannot do anything for God."

I must say a few words on the relations of retirement from business *with business*.

First, then, in retiring from business, *do not take
business with you.*

It is possible to come out of the world, and have
all its cares and objects still within you. It is not
the local withdrawment that is so important, but

the mental. Endeavour to leave secular concerns in secular places. Lock them up in the closed shop, the forsaken counting-house. This is necessary to the proper use of retirement. Even if your mind be perplexed and harassed, this may be the best thing to do; for it is not by poring over troubles and difficulties that we get to see the way out of them—the mind may lose its power of sight by too studious and anxious a gaze. Something is gained by a change of topic—and many a man has found on coming again and fresh to a trying problem, that he has easily solved it, whereas if he had not abandoned the endeavour for a season, it might have retained all its difficulty. Do not, then, bring the world with you into private life. Determine to resign it when you leave its scenes. With many, private life is as secular as business life. Wherever they are, their hearts are with their treasures. Whatever they do, they are thinking of their worldly work. Their only talk in the family and the social circle is talk savouring of commerce or politics. And even in the house of God they are planning and scheming, "buying and selling in the temple."

Do not bring the spirit of business into your retirements.

K

Many do; they have no taste nor power to do otherwise. All things are treated by them in a commercial temper—looked at from a commercial point of view. The highest and most sacred things are dealt with as matters of business—social life, morals, literature, religion. "Will it profit? Is there a demand for it? Will there be proportionate returns for the outlay?" Questions like these are apt to occur to the mind deeply engaged in secular affairs. But beware. Self-interest is not the greatest thing—we may be called to forego it for the sake of something better and nobler. The best things are to be sought and cherished on their own account and not on account of what they bring. And the best demands, the demands for knowledge and morality and religion, have not only to be supplied but often to be created. Especially is this mercantile mood displayed in our judgment and treatment of men. A man's worth is not his moral excellence but his pecuniary substance, and his respectability consists not in his title to be respected but in his success or good fortune in relation to property. When you come out of business, remember that you enter a sphere where other estimates should be formed, other tests applied. Let gold govern the things and places and systems in which and by which gold is made—but let it not invade provinces sacred to disinterested love, moral principle, spiritual holiness.

When retired from business, *look at business from those points of view which are accessible only in retirement.*

We cannot properly estimate our pursuits when actively engaged in them. It is often necessary to withdraw from an object in order to get a proper view of it—and we must come out of the world to see it clearly and fully. Anything may seem great, however small, if it be sufficiently near the eye— and the most insignificant objects of secular life are magnificent to him who is engrossed with them. Nor can we rightly judge of our own conduct in relation to them while we are dealing with them. It is when we are in the presence of spiritual realities, when we feel the powers of the world to come, when our hearts are opened to the generous influences of the love of Christ, when the mind is filled with ethereal sentiments, when the social affections are drawn out in peaceful pleasant exercise, that we are in a condition properly to appreciate the things of the world, and to pro- nounce sentence on our own deportment in connec- tion with them. And, therefore, when you have

come apart, look at what you have left behind, not
to perpetuate its solicitudes, but, in the coolness
and calmness of thought, and in the indulgence of
different feelings, to form a correct judgment of
the matters in which you have been concerned,
and of the spirit and temper in which you have
dealt with them.

When retired from business, *use your retirement,
at least in part, with a view to your return to it.*

I do not mean of course that you should make
your retirement a mere means of more effectually
prosecuting worldly pursuits.   I mean the reverse.
I mean that you should seek for a counteracting
influence to business—that you should "arm yourselves with the mind" most required by the condition and circumstances of your secular life—that
you should endeavour to acquire that in which you
have been most wanting, to strengthen what is
weak, and enlighten what is dark, and stimulate
what is slothful of spiritual principle.   It may be
that you have failed in the exercise of some moral
virtue, it may be that you have wronged some
brother, it may be that some particular sensibility
is in danger of being injured, it may be that some
care is becoming engrossing and benumbing—then
let your retirement be in part directed to this

matter. Let not sin lie upon your conscience—
confess it and seek its forgiveness. Examine and
heal the morbid portion of your nature. Be dili-
gent to obtain a supply of that peculiar strength
which your past history has taught you is chiefly
wanted. Don't let it be possible for you to go on
doing as you have done—yielding to the same
temptations—failing in the same duties—neglecting the same opportunities—or, what has been
occasional may become habitual, and that which it
might be easy to get rid of now, you may soon
find it difficult or impossible to get rid of. Retire
from business that you may return to it with cor-
rected estimates, worthier ends, and augmented
strength of soul.

II. I have spoken hitherto only of those retirements from business which may and should be obtained by Christians while engaged in business. I
did intend to speak at length on another point—
*that retirement from business which consists in a
final abandonment of it, in a complete resignation of
its concerns*—not that which takes place at death,
but that which takes place through a voluntary
act, in consequence of the obtainment of com-
petency, or the growth of infirmities, or the in-

fluence of other circumstances. I can, however, make only a few remarks on this subject.

My first remark is, *that retirement, in this sense may be a duty*.

It may be a duty, in order to give place to others. It is a selfish thing for a man to go on getting as much as he can, simply because he can. It behoves men, sometimes, to leave the lucrative sphere, that others may find employment and remuneration. And especially is this the case where the energies of the young are apt to be suppressed and their sense of responsibility weakened by the continuance of their elders in business. But the duty becomes still plainer when considered in relation to a man's own well being. If God have prospered secular diligence so that there is enough and to spare, it is a loud call to modes of activity and service that are impossible, to any great extent, in the heat and absorption of worldly pursuits. It was never the divine intention that those who do not need it should be evermore engrossed by perishing objects. I know that many find retirement a burden and a snare—many have returned to business after having left it, because they were oppressed by having nothing to do. But what a condemnation is this of their past life—what a re-

buke of their treatment of the immortal mind?
Nothing to do! And yet living in a world of mysteries? Nothing to do! And yet surrounded
with the images and works of God? Nothing to
do! And yet living after the race has lived six
thousand years, and Christianity been a divine gift
and power for nearly two? Nothing to do! And
yet the works of the mighty dead for centuries ex-
tant and full of glorious things and thoughts?
Nothing to do! And yet possessing a nature
which is the reflection of Deity, and the heir of
immortality? Nothing to do! and yet the world
in its sin and suffering calling for the utmost
tenderness of human compassion, and the utmost
activity of human energy? He who pleads that he
has nothing to do after business is abandoned—
*what has he been doing in the long years devoted to
its pursuits?*

When a Christian has retired from business, *he
should form some settled plan of life.*

He should not indulge in indolent repose—nor
leave his soul to the chance of accidents. Mischief,
morbidity, self-indulgence, trouble and annoyance
to others, will be sure to result if he do. If nothing
claim the healthful exercise of his faculties, he
should find or make something—remembering that

he is not approaching the end of his existence but
its transference to another state, its development
in a nobler sphere. The years that intervene between business and death should be employed in
cultivating and maturing powers that are to last for
ever—in purging the soul from the defilements
contracted in its past intimacy with secular affairs—
in attending to what has been neglected, in sup-
plementing what has been deficient—in fitting the
spirit for that world of service and enjoyment
where business will be unknown, and only its
spiritual essence and influence be felt to be of any
worth. Those years should be as "the prepara-
tion for the Sabbath." And especially should
they be devoted to the doing of good. Especially
should the leisure then possessed be redeemed by
active service in the Gospel of God's grace—in
imitating his example whose whole life was a sacrifice of love.

VII.

The Christian's Farewell to Business.

LUKE XVI. 9.

"And I say unto you, Make to yourselves friends of the mammon of unrighteousness; that when ye fail, they may receive you into everlasting habitations."

OUR subject to-night is, The Christian's Farewell to Business;—and the text appears to me a very suitable one, as it refers to the dismission from our earthly office—to our reception to the heavenly sphere—and to the relation between the use of what is now with the enjoyment of what is to come. To these topics I ask your serious attention.

I. *A Farewell imports a look behind.* What is there in the Christian's last look at the world?

It is a fact that that look *must* be taken. It is not possible to avoid it. We may avoid many things, but not that. Of the end of business we can have no doubt. If it end not before death, it will at death. Whatever its nature and its results, it will come to a termination. There may be many changes first, but that change will come. Let it be prosperous or adverse, it will cease. It is a tender thought. "The place that knows us now will know us no more." The people with whom we associate now will see us no more. The work which engages us now will be performed no more. You will go for the last morning to your shop and your counting-house. You will write for the last time in your ledger. You will appear for the last time in the mart and the exchange. And this last time is not a distant time. Many of you have seen your prime, some are in your decay. Oh! is it a fact—and shall you not give it place and pathos in your hearts? Do you engage in business as a thing to end, and end soon, or as an immortal thing? Let me beseech you to keep in mind the fact of its speedy termination. "I must leave it;"—then how inferior are its interests, seeing they will close. "I must leave it;"—then how foolish to make the parting painful by an excessive devotion to its pursuits. "I must leave it;"—then let me be in it as if I had to look on it from without and afar—freed from all the perverting and blinding influences of near objects and passionate feelings. "I must leave it, and leave it as a trust to give in my account;"—then let me walk before God in it, with an humble, anxious and conscientious solicitude, that as a steward I may be found faithful—and "at my failure be received to everlasting habitations."

When the end comes, there will be a tenderness in the adieu. Of course, there will be much to make a farewell pleasant. Business will be an object of not unmingled regret. Its end to many will be the end of distressing bodily fatigue and mental anxiety, of the painful stretch of physical and intellectual faculty, of feverish solicitude as to the issue of delicate and complicated tasks, of unquiet dependence on others whose wisdom and will may be at fault, of harassing cares and depressing disappointment, of an oppressive sense of responsibility, of keen anguish at the dishonesty and wrong of the selfish and dishonourable, of excitement bordering on distraction from the number and variety and extent of enterprizes, of perplexing moral difficulties, perilous moral temptations. We can imagine the delight with which the poor clerk bids adieu to the desk at which he has toiled monotonously through many a long day, on a salary that merely kept him in life to struggle with his lot. We can imagine the delight with which

the artizan bids adieu to the dark room in crowded
street and poisonous air, where, with no chance of
amendment, and no opportunity of recreation, he
managed to earn something less for a family of
souls than many of his brethren spent upon one of
the beasts that perish. We can imagine the delight with which the merchant bids adieu to a
business which has been so ramified and extended
as to press with exhausting force on both mind and
heart, following him to his hours and scenes of
retirement with besetting urgency, extracting all
the ease and sweetness of life, and making the
pillow itself a place of thorns. To these and others
there must be delightful relief in the summons to
depart.

But still, we say, there must be tenderness in
the adieu. *It is an adieu.* It is a parting from
that which has engaged the soul's best energies
and affections,—which has become connected in-
timately with its very nature,—which has become
to it a habit and a life,—to which, by reason of its
manifold associations, it has got to feel a sort of
personal regard,—yea, which has become almost a
kind of person, a second self, through the thoughts
and feelings and acts of which it has been organ

and instrument. For things do absorb, so to speak, a portion of our own being by long intercourse and use. Being the objects of deep and tender love, the contemporaries, companions, depositories, witnesses of many and varied thoughts— the ends, motives and means of volition—they are like things possessing life though lifeless, having souls though soulless. They have something for suggestion to almost all our meditations, for response to almost all our formal thoughts—and, being full of that of which we ourselves have been full in varied moods, they are reflections of our changeful states, mirrors of our inner and mysterious being. It is thus that the closet of the pious man becomes a holy place. It is instinct with a sacredness which no other spot in the universe can possess—for there he has wept, trembled at God's word, agonized in prayer, wrestled with God and prevailed. It is thus that the walk of the meditative becomes favourable beyond all other walks to deep and fruitful thought, for there many a finished and unfinished train of reflection is brought again to mind, and the very air breathes an influence soothing and gently stimulating. And it is thus that even secular business becomes a part by being

a counterpart of the man himself—or, at least, as
an outer garment of the soul, a house in which he
can dwell and feel at home.

But there are other sources of regret. Business
has been a source of *positive enjoyment*. It has
supplied a wholesome excitement. It has exercised
the active powers. To the thoughtful it has been
a ministration of truth. In intercourse with
others, in the use and application of the laws and
ordinances that govern mind and matter, and in
the development and impulse of their own nature,
which it has occasioned, they have had the materials of much useful thought, and the light of
more. In the gradual growth of enterprise and
the rewards of success, they have found objects
of pleasing hope and a source of deep gratification.
Their fellowship with others has helped to elicit
their own powers—in their fellow men they have
had an image and an influence revealing and affect-
ing themselves—while many a secular incident has
brought out beautiful and blessed tokens of latent
good in trust, affection, generosity, and high integrity.

Nor can we omit to remark that when the
Christian fails in death, he leaves, in business,
that which has been the channel and scene of

spiritual things. It is in business he has "exercised himself to godliness." The place of work has been the place of prayer. "There," pointing to one spot, can he say, "I poured out my heart to God in sweet and earnest supplication." "There," pointing to another, "I had thoughts that relieved and cooled my hot and angry spirit, raising me above the world, and enabling me to treat both its successes and its failures as very little things." "There," pointing to a third, "I obtained most unexpected deliverance. The needed interference was vouchsafed. The light burst upon my path, as out of darkness." "There," pointing to a fourth, "I gained the victory over a besetting sin; the force of temptation was broken. On the point of yielding, divine strength was perfected in me, and I triumphed by suffering, I gained in losing, I forewent profit but saved principle." And if business has thus been a path in which he has walked with God, if a book in which he has read his lessons, if a work in which he has served him, it cannot be without a tear that he leaves it even for better and nobler things. The tender thoughtful boy is touched with pathetic melancholy as he bids farewell to the school where he has spent the germinant years of youth, albeit

L

many a hard lesson and harder chastisement and the prospect of home and worldly life give him the joyous sense of freedom, and inspire him with hope and high ambition.

In some cases there are special causes of regret. When the young are removed from secular life just as they have entered it, and begin to realize the feeling of personal independence; when the strong and active are cut down in the midst of days and eager expectation; when the possessors of important secrets are withdrawn from scenes in which they might have brought to bear plans and theories full of fruit to themselves and to the world; when those are taken away on whom others are dependent, ere the opportunity of providing for their necessities has been afforded; when a growing and prosperous business has to be resigned to those who cannot work it with the requisite wisdom and energy; and when the dying are filled with worthy impulses and aspirations, regard prosperity as a means of usefulness, and meditate purposes eminently conducive to the welfare of mankind; in these cases, there are peculiar elements of sorrow in the departure from the present world, and with unusual pathos is the farewell bidden to the busy scenes of work and commerce.

II. Let us now contemplate the Christian *in his hope, in that bright prospect which is before him when he leaves the world,* as he looks forward to "the everlasting habitations" to which he will be "received" at his failure in death.

It has been my design, in these lectures, to describe, not the source of a Christian's principles, but their operation. But, as we are brought, to-night, into the presence of death and judgment, as we have to do with the saint on his entrance into glory; and, moreover, as this is the last lecture of the course; a few words on the ground of the Christian hope, that when we fail we shall be received to heaven, may be desirable.

That ground is *Christ.* It is not because we are by good works entitled to it that we can obtain an inheritance above. We cannot stand before God in judgment except as pardoned through the merits of the Saviour. And let me warn you here against a prevalent error. The virtues and charities of life are perpetually put in the place of Christ. Ask the men with whom you deal and mingle on what they rest their expectation of future happiness—and many of them will refer you to their honesty, their integrity in business, their social repute, their kindness to the poor. If these things be not alleged, they are really the grounds of hope. Now, this is a sore delusion. We do not disparage these excellences, far from it. So far as they go, they are to be regarded and honoured. But consider—they are not complete. There is another department which may be neglected—and has been neglected. These things belong to you as citizens of earth—by them your fellow-men are benefited—but you are creatures as well as companions, subjects of God as well as dwellers upon earth. And the charge of this book, which your own consciousness may ratify, is, that in respect to *God* you have been wanting. That law which requires you to love *Him* with all your heart and strength has not been fulfilled. I might take even lower ground. That law which requires you to love your neighbour as yourselves has not been fulfilled. And your business testifies to this fact. There might be obtained from it materials enough for your condemnation. If God were to try you by your secular works only, you would fail before him. There has not been *perfect* truth—*perfect* love—*perfect* integrity. And if not, then who can stand with the confidence of innocence in the presence of the great God and judge? Oh! believe me, that your only refuge is the cross— you must be "accepted in the beloved"—"you must look for the mercy of the Lord Jesus Christ unto eternal life"—"that eternal life must be the gift of God through our Lord Jesus Christ." " Found in him," you may meet death with composure, and even " rejoice in hope of the glory of God." When you "fail," then will you most succeed ; and your dismissal hence will be your reception to the skies.

This faith in Christ is always a principle of universal godliness. Christ dwells in the heart by faith—is "formed " in it,—we receive him in the power of his spirit,—he lives in us transforming, ruling, regulating our powers.

And, therefore, I remark, first, that though secular life closes at death, *the Christian retains all that made that life holy and noble.*

With many, business was an end—with him it was a means. With many, the thought, the care, the aim, the ambition, were all comprised in this outward world—with him the outward world was but a glass, a tool, a stepping-stone. The love of money and the love of that which money represents were not his principles of action. He worked as a servant of God ; he possessed as a steward of God ; he dispensed as an almoner of God. Faith in the invisible governed his dealings with the visible, enabling him to endure the adverse and enjoy the prosperous, guiding his estimates, and elevating his affections. Love to Him who is not seen was the spring and spirit of all his good deeds towards men. The pursuits of business were always but accidental shapes of spiritual principle—the words that told the inward man. He regarded life as a sphere in which he might fulfil the good pleasure of his Lord—not as a scene of self-gratification. He valued things without not according to what they were, but according to what they did, and enabled him to do. The value of life to him was a value which it derived from him. The world filled other men's hearts, his heart filled the world. What they were they were greatly made by it, what it was to him he greatly made it. He carried about with him in the grace of God, the key that unlocked it, the light that illustrated it, the power that wielded it. However barren it might be, he had "a well of water springing up to life everlasting"—however dead it might be, "his life was hid with Christ in God." When he fails, then, he keeps that which gave to business its highest worth and charm and use in the holy vitality of his soul. Not only does he survive—but everything most

valuable in life survives with him. Secularity was
but a dress, now laid aside—the wearer lives; a
work now finished—the worker lives. The worldly
man may bewail the loss of death, for his heart
was with his treasure, and his treasure was below
—and melancholy are the parting woes of the
sensual soul. The dying grasp — the clenched
fist unwilling to let go its gold—the soul clinging
to its poor perishing portion with the greater
tenacity as it is bidden to depart—is a distressing
sight. Hear men lamenting only that death has
cut short some prosperous pursuit—lamenting that
their hoards may not be preserved by their suc-
cessors; hear one regretting how the hearse will
cut up the gravel walk before his door; see another, on learning that his linen will be the per-
quisite of his nurse, clothing himself in rags just
before his death; and you have, in these extreme
cases, a fearful indication of the thoroughly worldly
man's spiritual state in dying. He was a soul,
but he cared only for the flesh and fleshly things,
and, now he is going, he is leaving behind all he
lived for, and is poor indeed. But the Christian
leaves only that which had an accidental worth,
and he takes with him the intrinsic excellence and
strength and glory of his earthly being. *He* is

received to everlasting habitations, and he is a new creature, a child of God, a temple of the Holy Ghost.

And while the Christian retains his principles, which made his business good and holy and happy, *those principles are transferred to a better sphere at death.*

They survive death, but that is not all. He is destined to no inactive, indolent existence. His joy was in work below, he will still be engaged above. The law of God was that he should labour on earth, it will be that he should labour in heaven. We cannot conceive of health or happiness apart from occupation, and are sure that in the glorious world to which we go there will be fitting exercise for our renewed and regenerated powers. It is not for us to say what it will be—perhaps we could not even appreciate, perhaps not now even understand it—but the blessed ordinance of service will be eternal, and, at death, we shall only exchange the lower for the higher sphere. The activity which here was the means of so much good, of acquisition, of enjoyment, of improvement, of usefulness, of glory to God, will evermore secure enlargement of mind and gladness of heart, will evermore minister to others, and evermore fulfil the pleasure of our heavenly Father. Were we to exchange the bustle and stir of life for a state of sleep or quiescence or indolent enjoyment, we might regret our departure from the world, notwithstanding its troubles and annoyances, but the holy and industrious energy which we expended in the days of flesh on earthly things will have a glorious scene and a glorious recompense in the kingdom of our Lord. And there we shall be engaged on objects of greater majesty and worth,—and there we shall serve under more inspiriting auspices,—and there we shall enjoy more powerful helps,—and there we shall achieve more magnificent results.   Dealing less with matter and more with the high realities of God and spirit—freed from the corruptions and infirmities of flesh and sin—no more oppressed by sorrow and failure—and full of light and full of love, our way will be prosperous, and we shall "do exploits." The things that sadden and weaken the soul here will give place to things only strengthening and gladdening. The depressed heart will be no more—the aching head no more— the trembling hand no more—no more the impracticable material and awkward tool—no more the dishonest servant and cruel creditor and fraudulent debtor—no more the blight destroying the harvest of anxious deeds—no more the cup dashed to pieces just as it was brought to the parched lips. There the weary cease from trouble—sickness, sorrow, tears, death have passed away—there is "free course" for all the activities of a holy nature—an everlasting work, done with joy unspeakable and richly recompensed.

The Christian, in failing at death, will not only be able to expect the continuance of holy activity in a better sphere—but *to connect his past with his future activity*.

He will take to heaven the principles that animated his secular life and blessed it—and he will take them as chastened and nourished and invigorated by his worldly work. Business is a discipline—in exercising the graces of the Spirit, it matures them. And all that it does in this way is done for ever. We lose nothing of the spiritual influence of secular pursuits. Every attainment is a reason of gracious recompense, and a means of further advancement. How this may comfort the heart in looking on the world. Does it demand patience, faith, trust, resignation, long-suffering, fortitude? Are these virtues called for every day? Can I "finish my course with joy" only as I display them? Do temptation and disappointment and wickedness and difficulty claim their exercise, bring them out, harden them, deepen them? Then, when I go to "everlasting habitations," shall I not rejoice in this service and discipline that had so blessed an action on my heart? It may be that the specific forms of these graces may not be wanted, may not be possible, in heaven. Where there is no difficulty, there may be no call for fortitude—and where no suffering, none for patience—and where no sin, none for long-suffering—but these virtues were only shapes of a general principle of holy life, accidental applications of an immortal power, and that has been fostered and strengthened by all that has called for them. The Jewish life in Canaan differed from Jewish life in the wilderness, but were not the people of God better prepared for the land of promise by the passage through the desert? David the king had very different duties and trials and responsibilities from David the shepherd, the outlaw, the exile, but was he not fitted for the throne by the lowly life and sore discipline that preceded its possession? And even so, the works and woes, the conflicts, the difficulties of secular business, in making necessary modes of religious action not required in heaven, confirm

and invigorate and perfect that essential holiness
of which heaven will be the unmerited reward, and
the everlasting sphere.   Faithfulness in regard to
the unrighteous mammon will fit for, and be
followed by, "the true riches."

Reed and Pardon, Printers, Paternoster Row, London.

Lightning Source UK Ltd.
Milton Keynes UK
UKHW022109160223
417164UK00024B/240